To you,
Keep believing —
you

ADVANCE PRAISE FOR *I STILL BELIEVE*

"This is a compelling, powerful story about Russ Taff's life. It'll blow your mind on many levels. He is sharing what probably many of you did not even know about his life. A very troubled childhood, and a battle with addiction, which many people have these days. The beauty about the story is that God is still in the business of redeeming people. And this is an extraordinary story of redemption."

—Michael W. Smith,
Christian Recording Artist

"I love Russ Taff. He's one of my favorite people and that wife, Tori, oh gosh. You know, he would be nothing without her. He wouldn't. I mean, really, she is a rock. I'd rather someone show me their scars than show me their trophies, and he's got six Grammy awards, but I bet you've never heard him say it. He's a legend and he just happens to be an alcoholic. And I've known that for years, and all those who love him have known that. And he has worked through it and it has been a process that I would not have wanted because it's a hard one."

—Mark Lowry, Christian
Recording Artist and Comedian

"I know of no one in the Christian music field who is loved as much as Russ is loved. And I think one of Russ' greatest gifts is he's still able to laugh at himself. I don't know of anybody with more humility, and maybe this is true because of pain, because character usually comes through pain. Seldom does character come through success. And you can't say Russ without Tori. This sweet little lady was just there the entire time, soft and gentle and yet as tough as somebody who really loves somebody needs to be in that situation. I don't think I know of anybody in our field who has been such an extender of grace than Tori."

—Bill Gaither, Southern
Gospel Music Legend

I STILL BELIEVE

RUSS AND TORI TAFF
WITH MARK SMEBY

POST Hill
PRESS

A POST HILL PRESS BOOK

ISBN: 978-1-64293-148-8
ISBN (eBook): 978-1-64293-149-5

I Still Believe:
A Memoir of Wreckage, Recovery, and Relentless Love
© 2019 by Russ Taff and Tori Taff
All Rights Reserved

Cover image by Ben Arrowood
Interior typesetting by Honeylette Pino and Sarah Heneghan

Post Hill Press, LLC
New York • Nashville
posthillpress.com

Published in the United States of America

*To Maddie Rose & Charlotte, the very best part of our story.
We still (and always will) believe in you.*

CONTENTS

FOREWORD

So as it turns out, writing a book isn't easy. We've been talking about doing this for a very long time because—at the risk of sounding pretentious—we believe that sharing our story could offer some hope to people who might be going through something similar to us. The challenging part has been that opening our private lives up for public consumption is more than a little bit scary. But even though our picture is on the cover and you're reading our words, this book is truly not all about us. Woven through every line and chapter is the relentless love and grace of God, who mourned every mistake, cheered every triumph, and absolutely refused to give up on us.

One of the hardest things to write about was Russ' childhood. We have no desire to disrespect or dishonor the memory of his parents, who, like all of us, were complex and multi-dimensional. Hurting, broken people can be loving and kind, yet still capable of causing a great deal of harm. The purpose of telling our truth is to unflinchingly shine a light on the devastating, long-term effects of trauma, abuse, and addiction—and bear witness to other hurting families that recovery, forgiveness, and restoration are truly possible.

We believe this is an important and timely conversation to have, especially among people of faith. Many of us are wrestling with issues that are too frightening and humiliating to admit to anyone and the sense of isolation can be overwhelming. Being told to pray more, memorize more verses, or attend more church services may be well-meaning advice, but it usually just drives people further into the shadows.

To anyone who is struggling with any kind of addiction, please know that God has never left your side. Even if you can't feel Him, even if shame is whispering that it's impossible to come back from the degrading, devastating mess you've made—God loves you more than you can imagine, exactly where you are right now. He's not waiting for you to get all cleaned up and shiny before He steps into your life. Truly believing that you are loved will be the foundation you need to rely on as you take steps toward your own recovery and redemption.

And to the person in a relationship with someone trapped in addiction, please know that as much as you want to, you cannot save your loved one from themself. That is God's job. It's easy to get lost in their pain and turmoil, often at the expense of your own sanity. Look for competent, compassionate people you can tell your story to who understand addiction. Let them share their experience, strength, and hope with you. There is help out there, we promise. You just have to hang on and keep fighting until you find it.

We know that God directed every single step on the path to our healing, and He consistently led us to gifted professionals who were uniquely trained and qualified to guide us through the process. And even in our darkest days He surrounded us with a small army of steadfast friends and family who carried us when we were too weary to walk, who made us laugh when we were too heartbroken to speak. We have been loved tremendously, and we can never say thank you enough.

With love, Russ & Tori

ONE

BEGINNINGS

I learned how to hide at an early age. I hid a lot. It served me well when I was a kid, protecting me from people and situations that weren't safe. But hiding became a way of life as the years progressed, and what started as self-defense, turned into self-offense.

I figured out as a small boy that people wanted to see a certain thing when they looked at me. When I sang, people treated me differently. They heard this big voice coming out of this emotional little kid, and they just melted. But even back then, deep down I felt completely unworthy of the praise and attention, even though I was starved for it. I saw that people responded to how my singing made them feel, so I learned to give them what they wanted. I hid behind the personae that made them happy, and it worked. Years later, by the time I was winning Grammy awards and topping the charts, I had been trotting out that facade for so long that I didn't even know if there was a real person behind it anymore. Turns out there was, but I had a whole lot of pain to go through before I found him.

My life has always had a certain yo-yo quality to it. Amazing opportunities would seemingly just be handed to me, then just as quickly, situations would arise that absolutely cut my legs out from under me. I'm not special—everybody's life probably feels like that. I never really trusted the good things because I knew bad ones had to be just around the corner. Trusting people was even harder. I knew how to make people like me, but it's quite another thing to actually let them in. Tori once said that my nickname should be "The Cheese" because like the "Farmer in the Dell" nursery rhyme says, I always stand alone. I'm not sure if that instinct to isolate was always within me or if it developed later when clinical depression really settled in. Either way, it's not exactly a building block to healthy relationships. And the craziest part was how after I finally pushed the people closest to me away, I was left with the one person I trusted least of all—me.

But here's what I love about God. Every single time I was just about to go under, just about to be crushed under the weight of my own self-hatred, guess what He used to reach me? People. Relationships. Connection. I was secretly convinced that I was just too fundamentally broken to deserve anyone's love. Maybe God took that as a personal challenge and was determined to change my mind because He just kept dropping the exact right people into my life at the exact right time. A family that took me in when I was seventeen. An evangelist that believed in me and gave me a job. Tori. It was like following a trail of human breadcrumbs—it just took me a little longer than most to make it out of the woods.

The biggest miracle to me is that, in spite of all the harsh religious rules and expectations I was raised in, I finally came to believe in a God who understands and forgives. One who takes an insecure young boy full of fear, hurt, and pain and begins to knock off those rough edges and form a man. These days I am standing and singing with more joy and freedom than I've ever had in my life.

But before I get too far ahead of myself, I want to go back to the early days. There are some things there that I have kept hidden my whole life. And I'm tired of hiding.

* * * * *

My grandfather on my mother's side had a farm in Arkansas. When the farm bellied up, he started running moonshine to make some money. When my mother was young, her job was to hide the moonshine. She would bury it in the yard and then go get it when someone would come to buy. My grandfather got caught when the sheriff started nosing around and found him running away from the moonshine still carrying two 20 lb. bags of sugar—a dead giveaway that he was making 'shine. He spent six months in the county jail before deciding to move to California after hearing about work available in the shipyards in Los Angeles. Gradually, my grandmother and most of their six children joined him there.

My mother was in Hot Springs working at a little diner called the Baby Elephant Cafe when she met my father. He was in the army, stationed at the big Army Navy Hospital there. She was really shy when Dad first tried to talk to her, so he pretended he had a wife and asked Mama to please help him pick out a present for her. Once she got comfortable with him, he told her he wasn't really married and soon they started dating. It wasn't long after they got married that Mama and her siblings continued the family migration out to California. Eventually they settled in the San Joaquin Valley, which has some of the richest farm soil in the world and plenty of jobs available harvesting fruit. I was born November 11, 1953 in

Farmersville, California, the fourth of five sons to Joe and Ann Taff. Even though I was raised in California, my roots will always be in Arkansas.

Most of my childhood was spent in church. We were old line Pentecostal. There were no newspapers, no TV, no magazines, no Christmas trees, no participating in sports at school—basically no *anything* that would look like we were "partaking of the world." It was supposed to make us more holy, I guess.

We were in church Tuesday night, Thursday night, Saturday night, Sunday morning, and Sunday night. What pulled me in and held me was the music. Mama had a strong alto voice and she would sing with her four sisters. And I'm not just saying this because it was my mother—they were great. I mean, they were really, really good. They were invited to be on the popular country music radio and TV show, *Louisiana Hayride*, but my grandpa was afraid that men might hit on them, so he wouldn't let them go.

Music was a such a big part of their lives. Mama said they would be walking home from school, and they'd just start singing, complete with all of the harmonies. It was so magical watching them sing, it made me want to do it too. When I was three, my mama stood me up on the altar and I squeezed my eyes shut tight and sang my first solo. When I finished, there were a whole lot of loud *Amens*, and I got back pats and hugs all the way back to my seat. A couple of people even pressed some change into my hand. I think I ended up with about forty-five cents. All that positive attention and money, too? A career path was born!

We never took a real vacation because our summers were spent with Dad preaching revivals for a month in Arkansas and Missouri. So, our "vacation" was four weeks of church. I remember my mother asking Dad one time, "Why don't we go to the beach or something?" And he said, "What would we do *there*?"

Dad just loved to preach so much, he was a preaching machine. And he was good at it. That was his golf, his fishing—that was everything to him. He was a very charismatic man, and even with just an eighth-grade education, he was a great communicator. I think when he was in the pulpit, that was the only time he felt good about himself. He was saving folks from hell, so maybe God wouldn't be mad at him for at least as long as the sermon lasted.

Our church was very small, maybe thirty people, and they were mostly family. But during the months when it was fruit-picking time, attendance would increase by ten or so with the migrant workers who would join us for worship. But because we were all mostly relatives, there would always be a lot of arguments that would lead to a church split, and I'd come in on Sunday and there would be twelve people. And then somebody would start feeling guilty, they'd make up, and then the next service we would have twenty-five.

Eastside Tabernacle was a wild church. None of the women shaved their legs. They didn't wear makeup, and believe me, they needed it. They also thought putting on deodorant or cologne was wrong, so after church when those ladies had shouted and danced themselves sweaty, of course *that's* when they wanted to hug little Russie. They'd wrap their big old arms around me and I'd hold my breath. My cousin and I dated the Baptist girls across town because they looked good. Maybe they weren't allowed to dance, but they could wear makeup.

There was a guy in Daddy's church, and he was a runner, though they don't really do this much anymore. My dad would preach the congregation into a lather and this guy would get so wound up he'd just jump up and run down the aisle to the backdoor. And he had it down where he would get to the back door, turn the knob and open the door all in one motion, and start running circles around the outside of the church, shouting hallelujah and speaking in tongues. I know the neighbors thought we were just lunatics. But he had it down to an art.

When you're nine years old and all this stuff is going on, I'll tell you one thing, you sure never went to sleep in church! You just never knew what was going to happen. One Sunday night, this guy got all fired up and he tore out running. He reached the door at full speed, turned that handle…and the door didn't open. It was locked. He smacked his head so hard he knocked himself out. I busted out laughing.

Mother pinched me on my arm and said, "Shut up, shut up."

I said, "Mom, that's the funniest thing I've ever seen," and I couldn't stop laughing. So, she took me outside and I got a whipping, but it was almost worth it. The running guy always said he was just doing what the Lord led him to do. I always tried to picture God sitting up in heaven, looking down and thinking, "You know what, I would really enjoy it if that guy would jump up and run around the church a few times." I don't know if God liked it that much or not, but I know I did.

* * * * *

My Dad got saved at a little church in nearby Cameron Creek a couple of years before I was born. He never really talked much about his life before he became a Christian, but from what I can gather he had been a hard drinker during his army years. That all stopped when he got saved. He felt called to the ministry and started preaching at Eastside Tabernacle.

When I was seven, Dad was working at his job building farm machinery and a piece of welding slag flew into his eye. It was a painful injury, and the doctor sent him home with a supply of pain medication which, unbeknownst to everyone including Dad, triggered his addiction again. Mom must have been a little leery of the pain pills because she kept them in her purse and doled them out to Dad as prescribed. One day he came out to the backyard where I was playing and pulled me aside. With tears in his eyes, he begged me to go get his pills out of Mama's purse and bring them to him. I said, "Dad, that would be stealing," but he said that this time it would be okay. The desperation on his face scared me and I just kept repeating, "I can't do that." His face turned dark and angry. He said he couldn't believe I wouldn't help him. I felt so torn—I wanted to please him, but I knew it was wrong. I started crying and ran off. And as soon as the prescription for the pain pills ran out, he picked up the bottle again.

I was clueless about all of this until the Sunday night service. Dad didn't show up at church and Mom sent me down the block to the house to find him.

When I walked into the house, I could hear a strange noise coming from the back bedroom. Somebody was singing a song I'd never heard before in a slurred, fuzzy voice. I froze in my tracks because I thought someone had broken into our house. But it was Dad, sprawled out across the bedspread, staring up at the ceiling and singing. I had never seen anyone drunk in my life, I didn't even know what it was or how you got that way. It just looked like something was wrong with him. So, I ran back to the church as hard and fast as I could go to try to get him some help. I can still remember the look of fear on Mom's face. And that's how it began.

Our life swung from one extreme to another. My father would be in the pulpit preaching a hard holiness gospel one day, then another day he would just disappear. He would go out and park his truck somewhere and drink until he passed out. Sometimes he'd be gone two or three days. My brothers and I would have to go out and try to find him. A lot of times he would be passed out in some farmer's orchard and we would bring him home. If he wasn't ready to sober up yet, he'd lay around the house drunk, sometimes for a month, barely eating a thing.

It was scary because he turned into someone I didn't know. When he was drunk out of his mind, he called Mama all kind of obscene names. We didn't know those words, we'd never heard that kind of language in our house before. Eventually he would sober up, and then he'd cleverly maneuver his way back into the good graces of Mom and the church. We'd all be wary, but hopeful. Until the next time it happened.

My older brothers started leaving home. The oldest, Billy Joe, got married. Marvin got drafted and went to Vietnam, thirteen months later Danny was sent there, too. So, for a lot of years, it was just my little brother, Earl, and I left at home with my parents. I literally became my younger brother's parent at twelve years old because Mom and Dad were both working long hours. I would make sure Earl did his home-work, that he had money for lunch at school, that we had enough food at home. We ate a whole lot of canned soup and government cheese.

We did have a safe place, though. Mom's mother, Grandma Mattie, was my anchor. She would babysit me and Earl sometimes. She knew something about the chaos that was going on at my house, and when things would get nuts, she'd kind of quietly step in. For some reason she and I just really connected.

Grandma Mattie was very Pentecostal, with this amazing silver hair that went below her waist. She loved to sing and had a great voice like my mom. I have such vivid memories of sitting on the porch with her, watching her comb her hair out and then rolling it up in a bun and pinning it on her head. She never would call herself a preacher, because of course women couldn't be preachers in our denomination, but when she came to church she would always testify during testimony service. She would just start walking up and down the aisle, preaching, getting louder and louder, adding more emotion. People would start worshiping, praying, dancing in the spirit, and speaking in tongues. Her favorite hymn was, "Lord, I Want To Go Home." As she sang, becoming more and more intense, twirling and spinning, the bun on her head would just come apart.

From the day I walked into the house and found Dad drunk, it was like a stick of dynamite was put under our house. Our lives exploded. But I could always go to Grandma's house. She had three very close friends and they quilted all day long. They would start at ten in the morning and go until four or five in the late afternoon. They had a big square wooden frame that would hold the quilting fabric in place, and they would lower it down and all of them would pull up a chair and begin to sew and chat. Me and Earl would get under it and act like it was a tent.

Grandma Mattie was steady, solid, and she loved me. She let me be a kid. She let me be scared. She listened to me talk. She told me that everything would be okay, that dad didn't mean to do what he did. But when you're a kid, that's difficult to understand.

When Daddy would rage against Mom, Earl and I would be so terrified that we'd hide underneath our bunk bed. I would push Earl up against the wall and lay in front of him because I was so afraid Dad was going to come in. We didn't know what else to do. He didn't ever hit Mom, but it always sounded like he might. I was just a kid, but I decided I could take on Dad if I had to in order to protect Earl from getting hurt. From under the bed we could hear him slurring and cussing. It wasn't my dad. I didn't know this guy, but he was scary—very scary.

Daddy preached a hard-line gospel that no one could live up to. Not even himself. He would just push himself and push himself, constantly working. I've never seen anyone work so hard for Jesus. His sermons would usually be about how we need to do better, do more. *We're not doing it right, so we need to fast more, pray more.* Then after months and months of wearing himself out, he would just disappear. We'd go out and find him, or sooner or later he'd come staggering back home. When you're living with that kind of addiction, it's almost like a demonic force comes into your house. Mama would be completely consumed with him, so angry but at the same time, so happy that he came home alive. One time he left and checked into a cheap hotel. He was so drunk that he fell and hit his head badly. If the maid hadn't come in that morning, he would have bled to death.

What is amazing is how, after a while, this all becomes normal. And you start recognizing the patterns. Dad would preach Sunday morning and Sunday night, go visit the sick, and pray for people in the hospital. On top of that, he worked long hours six days a week at his job building farm machinery. Day in, day out, providing for his family and running himself ragged for the Lord. Eventually, we'd feel the tension start to build in the house. He'd get kind of short and irritable with everybody. And then he wouldn't come home. Mama would pray and cry, terrified of what she knew was going to happen. And, of course, a small boy of eight or nine doesn't know how to provide comfort. So, you just feel abandoned because there is no mother now and there is no father—they are both so absorbed in this drama that happens over and over and over again.

After enough of these episodes, the church voted my dad out because you can't have a drunk pastor. My uncle, who was taking over the church, pulled me aside and said, "Russell, this means you can't come here anymore either."

And I said, "Uncle, I haven't done anything wrong."

Then he said, "I know, but your dad's not welcome, so you're not welcome either." It broke my heart. The shame of what Dad had done was transferred to me, even though I wasn't the one messing everything up.

One of the rules of our house was that you couldn't talk about anything that happened *within* the family to anyone *outside* of the family. I spent the night at the house of a friend from church and offhandedly told him that my parents had an argument at breakfast. When I got home the next morning, my mother was waiting for me. She began to rage at me for telling somebody that they had an argument. She started taking books off the shelf and throwing them at me. And then she came over with her fists and just started punching me like it was a boxing match. I just curled up in a fetal position against the wall while she continued kicking and kicking, screaming, "You don't tell anybody what goes on in this family." I had to wear long sleeve shirts to school, so nobody would see the bruises.

Years later, during one of my visits to a treatment center, I learned about something called "covert incest," also known as emotional incest. According to the professionals there, it's not physical touching, but the dynamic is that a parent looks to a child for the kind of emotional support, comfort, and even decision-making that would normally be provided by another adult. It's almost like turning your child into your spouse. It's incredibly confusing. By the time I was ten years old, it began. I don't know why my mother picked me, I had three older brothers. But they all got out of there as quickly as they could.

She started coming to my room and would just dump everything on me. I would have to sit on the side of the bed and listen to her telling me how scared she was, how angry she was at my dad. Telling me that we probably were not going to be able to meet the house payment this month and could lose our house. She'd even confide in me about their sex life and how bad it was. I had no idea what I was supposed to do with all this information; I was just a kid. It made me feel like our already shaky home life was even more out of control.

One day I said to her, "I wish he would just leave."

She backhanded me, busting my lip, saying, "He's your father, you have to respect him."

So, I learned to just sit there and listen because I couldn't respond. When she was done, she'd leave and go back to her bedroom and fall asleep. I was left sitting there with all this confusing, grown-up information that I had no way to process. And I was terrified, so unsure of what to do. I knew I couldn't fix it. This continued until I left home.

During those difficult early teen years when I was carrying all these heavy secrets, I had a place where I could escape—it was the church. Even though we'd been kicked out, I still had a spare key and would go down there around eleven o'clock at night. Nobody would even notice I was gone, because the whole family system had basically collapsed. At first it was scary because it was dark, and I certainly didn't want anyone to see lights on in there. But toward the front of the church was a desk with a small lamp on it. I would walk down the aisle in the dark and turn on that little light. And I would just sit on the altar and talk to Jesus. Through my tears I'd say, "I don't know what to do. I don't know what to do." Sometimes I'd stay there an hour, sometimes less. But it was a place where I could finally tell somebody about the pain, the anger, and all of those jumbled up, conflicting feelings. I hated how we were living, but I had to protect the secrets. I hated what mom and dad were doing to us, but I loved them, too. I was afraid of them, but I was loyal to them.

Those late-night church visits started a relationship between me and Jesus that became very strong. Eventually, not only was He my Savior, but He was someone I could talk to. Sometimes it was like a prayer, and sometimes it was just me telling Him, "I wish I could leave, and go someplace else to live, but I don't know where to go." The turmoil between our family and the church would cause extended family members to turn and walk the other way when they saw me coming down the sidewalk. My aunts and uncles wouldn't even say hello to me. There's no way for a kid to know what to do with all this. You certainly couldn't take it to the pastor, since he's the one causing all the chaos.

When I got into the ninth grade, I made the honor roll, which was unheard of in our family. I studied very hard, wanting them to be proud of me. But Mom and Dad were so preoccupied with their own world, they were oblivious to mine. They would never come to anything I was involved in, like a school play or a swim meet. One day I had swim practice, so I had to stay late and ended up missing the bus. Dad had to take off work an hour early to come get me, and I knew he'd be upset about that. I saw him pull up to the practice, and even though he never got out of the car, I could see him watching. I swam my heart out because he was watching. I got in the car hoping that he saw me swim, and the only thing he said to me was, "You ought to lose some weight." That was it.

To an impressionable kid, hearing your parents say things like "*You're not worth the bullet to shoot you with*" or "*Why can't you be smart like your cousin?*" or "*You're not worth the salt that goes on your bread*" can cause real and lasting damage. Because you believe them. The sad thing is, I really believe that Mom and Dad were raised the same way. They didn't know any different, they were just passing onto us what had been done to them. But what happens as you begin to get older, is that those negative messages are so strong and have been repeated so often that they leave a dug-out ditch in your brain. They convinced me that I wasn't as smart as everybody else, and I wasn't worth much to anyone—that was just who I was. I read a quote from Garrison Keillor once that said, "Everything you said went in one ear and right down my spine."

It's strange, but even in the middle of all that family dysfunction, we would still always sing. The music kept me sane, it seemed to be a valve that released a lot of the tension. I started singing with my four brothers, just like my mother with her four sisters. We would wait for a new Statesmen record to come out, or the Blackwood Brothers, and we would learn their songs and sing them at church.

Sometimes my oldest brother Billy Joe would come in my room before I went to sleep and tell me to close my eyes and picture myself singing in front of thousands of people.

Night after night he did that. I'd never heard of terms like "casting a vision" or "visualizing," but that's pretty much what we were doing.

Mama taught me how to play guitar when I was eleven, and I threw myself into it. When I would get home from school, my world became playing my acoustic guitar and singing, then putting Mama's quartet or black gospel records on the stereo and laying on the floor with my head between the speakers, tears rolling down my cheeks. Mahalia Jackson, Jake Hess, The Five Blind Boys of Alabama—that music spoke to me. It certainly didn't fix everything, but it would take my mind away for a while.

When I would talk with Jesus down at the church at night, I would ask Him to show me how to be a better singer, show me how to take what I felt inside and express it in song. My mom would always say, "When you sing you need to reach way down. Tap into that deep place where you're combining your spirit, soul, and body with the Holy Spirit." I wanted to feel that intensity, and I wanted the people listening to me to feel it, too.

When I sang in church, Dad and Mama would watch me, and I got a little taste of the attention I had been craving from them for so long. Unfortunately, my dad couldn't stand not being the center of attention. So, when I started really shining and getting praise from the congregation, he'd get incredibly jealous. It started a dance between he and I that lasted until I left home—it was so confusing to me. I felt like I was being trotted out in front of Dad's congregation like a show pony, but if I did well and the Holy Spirit moved, he would emotionally punish me. He would not even acknowledge me or make eye contact for a couple of days. I eventually learned how to just shut him out, but it always hurt. I even said to him once, "It feels like you're trying to destroy me."

He and my mama never complimented me. They were raised with the misinformed attitude that compliments were dangerous because they could make a person get a big head, so they wouldn't ever say anything about my singing. I was starving for them to tell me that I was doing a good job because I *thought* I was, but they never did. So, I started doubting my gift, wondering if I was just deceiving myself. Even when someone from church would tell me I had done well, it didn't matter. I really only wanted to hear it from my dad.

When I was fifteen and Dad had fallen off the wagon and been kicked out of the church again, we moved from California to Arkansas. There was a church there that Dad used to hold revivals in during the summer that said he could come back and be their pastor, even though they knew what had been going on with him. I was the one who had to finally step up and say that yes, we were going to move, since both of my parents were incapable of making any decisions. Mama had slipped into a deep depression and Daddy was usually intoxicated.

We had a friend offer to drive Daddy back to Arkansas with me, Earl, and Mom. So, we gathered up the essentials, and I made a pallet in the back of the station wagon for Dad. He was drunk out of his mind. We carried him out of the house and loaded him up in the back of the station wagon like a Christmas tree, tied some suitcases on top, and started driving two thousand miles to Hot Springs, Arkansas. When we got there, the church people helped us find a little house to rent. Dad sobered up and did his best to try to change for this whole new group of people who were willing to accept him as their pastor. And for two years he really tried. Then he relapsed and had to leave again.

I don't hold anything against him now. I truly don't. He was caught in the grip of something he didn't understand and couldn't control. People did not talk about this stuff openly, it was just our family's dirty little secret. Well, not very secret because sooner or later, Dad would publicly humiliate himself by staggering down the sidewalk or getting picked up by the police again and we'd be the talk of the town. There wasn't any Oprah talk show or internet searches back then to help explain all the different maladies that the human body and mind go through. Alcoholism wasn't considered a medical disease, it was just *sin*, pure and simple—and if you'd just get right with God, it would go away. Unfortunately, I ended up carrying that shame and lack of information into my own adult life.

In spite of the lack of encouragement and the ever-growing insecurities, I knew deep down that God had given me this voice not to be squandered, but to be used. I wanted to be excellent because I saw how people were moved when I sang. Even if my dad couldn't see that, I knew God could.

* * * * *

Before that two-year stint in Arkansas ended, I had put a little band together with some of the guys at the church. We called ourselves the Sounds of Joy. James Hollihan, Jr. played guitar, Doug Anderson was the drummer, Ronnie Vanderslice was the bass player, Charlie Davis played keyboards, Bobby Mason sang harmony, and I sang lead.

My buddy James was the best guitar player I had ever heard—still is, in my opinion. His background couldn't be more different than mine. His dad had a jazz combo that performed in nightclubs around Hot Springs, and underage James had cut his musical teeth playing alongside his dad at places like The Vapors and Maxine's. There was no way I could've known back then what an integral part of my life and music career this young man would be. Over the years of playing and writing together, we became musical soulmates. Onstage, it was like we read each other's minds. My friend Marshall Chapman used to laughingly call us "the gospel Mick Jagger and Keith Richards." My best vocal performances ever are on the records James produced with me because he knows my voice inside and out better than anyone on the planet, except Tori. I truly believe he is one of the reasons I've had such a long run in the music business. He said one time that he thought the only musical stones we left unturned were opera and polka music. Every time I wanted to explore a different sound, he was always right there, egging me on.

With a van and a small trailer for all our equipment, the Sounds of Joy began to go around Arkansas trying to reach our generation for Jesus. This was 1970 when there was no such thing as contemporary Christian music. So, my band started taking Beatles songs and rewriting them: "I want to hold God's hand…I want to hold God's hand!" It was so bad. Or Grand Funk Railroad's "I'm Your Captain," was changed to "Jesus our captain, Christ our captain." We were always looking for material we could play that didn't sound like it came out of a hymnal. That's what prompted me to start writing.

It was during this time that the Jesus Movement started to break out here in the States, and I had never experienced anything like that. I'd love to see it again before I die. It was a massive revival, a phenomenon. There were articles in *Time* magazine and stories on the national television news about this spiritual awakening were sweeping the country.

Nobody was using our church on Monday nights, so I asked if we could use it. I had begged our school principal for months to let the Sounds of Joy do two songs during an assembly, so when that happened, I invited everyone to come to our little church on Monday night for more music. We had a pretty good crowd the first night because they'd never heard music quite like that before. But by the second Monday, it was beyond full—people were standing outside the church, six or seven people deep. We'd have the windows open and speakers outside so everyone could hear.

I'd never really considered myself a preacher, but I would quote John 3:16 and talk about it a little bit. "For God so loved the world, that he gave his only begotten son. That whosoever believeth in him shall not perish but have eternal life." Then I would ask, "If anybody here would like to receive Christ, come on forward." Every Monday night the altar would be completely full.

During my last year in high school, guys would come up to me and say, "Russ, how do I find Jesus?" and I would pray with them in the locker room, the study hall, anywhere. Walking home from school people would just ask, "Tell me how to find Jesus. Tell me how to find Jesus." As a result, a great revival broke out in Cutter Morning Star High School. The year we graduated, they said 85 percent of the student body professed a belief in Jesus. I'd never seen anything like that, where the power of God moved so profoundly.

Me and the boys decided to get creative and come up with other ways of doing outreach. We tried to raise enough money to bring The Imperials, a popular Christian group, to our town. We didn't know how to get Love Song or Larry Norman, but The Imperials had just started promoting their latest album *Time To Get It Together*. Kids who wouldn't usually listen to quartet music were responding to this new sound.

We raised 1,500 dollars from car washes and assorted fundraising efforts to have them come. They let our little band play for twenty minutes before they came on. We had also learned the song that we knew The Imperials always ended their concerts with, "Old Gospel Ship," hoping they would call us up on stage with them to do the finale. I was prepared. I had brought a camera and asked Bud Smedley, "When I get up there, please take some pictures of me with The Imperials." We started singing and Bud, who doesn't like to draw attention to himself, stands up quickly, takes a picture, and sits back down. I was trying to get his attention, mouthing to him, "Take some more shots!"

After the concert, I took the film to Kmart to be developed. Three days later when the pictures came back, he had only taken one picture. And it was a picture of nine guys all from the waist down. My one time to be on stage with The Imperials, for crying out loud, and it was captured forever as nine random pairs of legs.

After high school, I felt like I needed to go to Bible school to get some training. The band graciously let me go and continued without me. I had heard about Christ for the Nations Institute in Dallas, so I went with my friend Harry Browning, also a musician with whom I had been in a few bands. I was prepared to beg the school to let me work to pay for the tuition since I didn't have anything when I arrived. Incredibly, Harry stepped up at registration and said, "I'll pay for it." It just floored me.

Harry and I got a room together in one of the dorms and worked cleaning the local McDonald's at four o'clock in the morning before our eight o'clock classes would start. I was only able to stay for one semester.

"Russ, you've got to come home," my mom pleaded with me on the phone.

"What happened?" I knew, but I had to ask.

"It's your father."

When I got back to Hot Springs, not only was my family in shambles again, but the church had shut down the Monday night band outreach. We used to take our van down to the park and ask people, "You want to hear a concert?" and just bring them back with us. The old-line church folks couldn't deal with the fact that boys with long hair and girls wearing shorts and halter tops were coming in right off the streets. They also didn't like the music, they said it was too loud and "worldly." When I found out that they shut it all down, it completely broke my heart. Our sacred little flock was scattered. I really cried over that one.

Meanwhile, since my dad had relapsed as usual and been asked to leave the church, the only thing my parents knew to do was to leave town. And the only place they knew to go was back to California. I desperately wanted to stay. I just couldn't do the dance anymore. I felt like if I didn't get off the crazy carousel of my parent's dysfunction, I was going to implode. There really wasn't anything for me in Hot Springs, but some survival instinct deep down inside was telling me to make the break now.

To help me through the days after my family left Arkansas, God sent me two angels. One was my English teacher and another was the most beautiful girl I had ever seen, who at the time was dating the quarterback of the football team. These two ladies became the strongest influences and greatest champions in my life. I can't wait to tell you all about the gorgeous babe that I fell in love with, and of course, she'll share her side of the story. You will fall in love with her, too.

But first, let me tell you about Mama June.

TWO

FINDING FAMILY

I met June Smedley during my senior year of high school. We had just moved to Hot Springs and she was my English teacher. It was her first year as a teacher, and she knew right away that I wasn't good at nouns and verbs, even though I loved to write. She was also the Senior Sponsor, which meant she was constantly doing outside activities with us—a trip to Florida, plays, fundraisers, parties at her house. There was a lot more interaction on a personal level with the students than you see nowadays.

She told me she had been a Christian education director and youth pastor at a church near Hot Springs. So, I asked her to come speak to our Monday night group at church, which she did several times. I loved her kids, too. Stuart was eleven and Kimmie was nine, and I could tell they looked up to me.

While I only ended up being at Christ For the Nations for a semester, I would write lots of letters home to June and Bud while I was there, as they were starting to feel more like family than my own. The school was very strict about us only reading the King James version of the Bible. And at this time, the Living

Bible had just come out and was becoming popular. In one let-
ter I wrote, "Read your Bible. King James version if possible."

Mama June wrote back and said, "Why do I have to read
the King James version?"

I said, "I don't know, but that's what they told me down
here. Just be careful with that Living Bible."

Mama June was so compassionate toward me. We talked
a lot about my family—how I had to cover for my dad, how
I was the one that would go out and get him when he would
drink and pass out in a field somewhere, how my father
needed me to cover for his sin.

My body began reacting to all the stress and tension at
home, with my back breaking out in sores and my hands
turning red and swelling. I even went to the doctor, telling
him I didn't know what was wrong with my body. He said,
"Could this be a venereal disease?" And I said, "I'm a virgin!"
Then he said, "Boy, whatever's going on in your life, you better change it." So, it was an act of desperation for me. I felt
like if I didn't get away from the pain and chaos, I'd die.

One night at church, my mother was talking to Mama
June and said they were moving back to California, but that I
had wanted to stay in Arkansas. "If only we had some family
he could stay with here, because I just can't stand to go off
and leave him by himself," my mother said. To which, Mama
June said, "Well, he could stay with us." That sealed the deal,
taking care of two birds with one stone—my mother needing
to know that I was going to be taken care of, and me, needing
to be rescued from my family.

I always felt guilty that I stayed in Arkansas and Earl
didn't. He was such a sensitive, gentle soul. He finished up
his sophomore year and then went with my parents back
to California. I should've asked if Earl could stay with the

Smedleys, too. But I didn't. I wasn't sure they could take in both of us, and I was afraid to risk losing my only hope of getting out. And I have carried that guilt with me, even to this day. The family curse of addiction landed squarely on Earl and he didn't have any defense against it. It was like he was missing a protective layer of skin, and his emotional nerve endings were right there on the surface. He carried the same negative self-image that my brothers and I did, and he sunk back down into what felt familiar to him. He never moved away from my parent's house, the real world was too big and scary for him. And tragically, at the age of forty-five—after probably not living a sober day since leaving Arkansas at seventeen—his body gave up. I know in my heart that his death was really a long, slow, painful suicide.

Moving in with the Smedleys changed my life. I got to see what a "normal" family looked like. They loved each other, it was uncomplicated and real. They liked hanging out together. We went on camping trips in an old school bus, and we sang in the car on the way to church. Everybody was valuable. Everybody was important. One of the main reasons that I'm still married today is because at that crucial time in my life, I finally got to experience a healthy family.

But it didn't always feel comfortable. I wasn't sure exactly how this kind of family system worked. When I felt insecure, I'd revert to some of the emotional mind games I'd grown up with, but they didn't work in this family. If they got mad at each other they'd talk it out and move on. Nobody pouted and punished, nobody raged and threatened. It was also the first time in my life that somebody saw me and my talent and cast a vision of a bigger world for me to get involved with. At the time, I had no idea what I wanted to do with my life. We had to fill out a form at school that asked what we want to be when we grow up. I just wrote "mechanic" because Daddy worked on cars and welded, and I thought, well, I guess I'll do that too. But June heard me sing and felt like there was something there.

She took me to a lady named Hettie Lou Brooks, a music teacher. She played the piano while I sang. I noticed that tears were just falling down her face. She said, "I've never heard anybody sing like he does." June and Hettie started scheming about ways they could help me.

Hettie and Mama June got me enrolled at Henderson State College in Arkadelphia. Unbelievably, June and her husband Bud sacrificially offered their whole savings account of 273 dollars to pay my tuition.

The music instructor there said that in all his years teaching, he had never had a student with as much pure natural talent. Obviously, I was very pleased with all this encouragement. But college wasn't for me—their music program was training people to teach music and I wanted to perform music. All the classes and homework, not to mention the expense of it all, got in the way of the ministry and singing that I wanted to be doing.

* * * * *

When I returned home from school, I continued playing with the Sounds of Joy, constantly trying to find new opportunities to minister. Hettie and Don were just starting up a new church and they asked if I'd be willing to be the youth and music pastor. It was going to be in the barn of their ranch with horses, fishing, and such. During the summer it was a camp, and kids from all over the United States would come and stay for a one-week or two-week program.

Hettie said to me, "Why don't you have a youth retreat?" We started advertising it as a two-day weekend for youth, starting on Friday afternoon and ending on Saturday.

I didn't know many people in the area, so I started going door to door to find people who might want to come to our church. On my first visitation, I was talking to a young man and his mother on the front porch. I was trying to be nice and casual, simply inviting them to church sometime. In the middle of the conversation, I turned and my foot got caught on a planter and fell over flat on my face right there in the front yard. I wasn't cool at all, but I was on a mission.

TORI

I was in high school in 1973. My parents, Don and Alexine Timm, had moved to Hot Springs from Little Rock a couple of years before because Daddy had taken over the management of Brandon's Furniture Store. I'm the youngest of their six kids, and we're a wildly diverse bunch full of strong personalities and opinions. Mama's family was French and Daddy was of German descent, so we're equal parts passion and stubbornness, with a side order of off-the-wall humor. Also, apparently when we're together we all talk at the same time, with lots of interrupting and overlapping. This was made abundantly clear the first year somebody showed up at Christmas with a personal camcorder and filmed us. Our family motto is "You lose your breath, you lose your turn." Carolyn, Matt, Joel, Jonathan and Liz—I'm absolutely crazy about every single one of them.

Liz, who is three years older than I am, had been going to a little church that had started as a Bible study. She heard about a youth retreat being planned and wanted someone to go with her. I didn't really want to go, but she talked my parents into thinking it would be a wonderful bonding experience for two sisters and we went. The year before, I had made that important transition from "I was raised in a Christian family" to embracing my faith as my own, but that didn't necessarily mean I was thrilled about the idea of giving up a whole weekend to spend with people I didn't know singing "Kumbaya" around a campfire. I perked up a little when I realized the retreat was being held in at Brookhill Ranch, a beautiful farm with horses and lakes that was a kid's camp in the summer.

When I walked into the main pavilion, people were all over the place eating and talking. I saw a couple of friends I knew from school, so we hung out together. And then I noticed Russ. He was in the middle of a large group of kids, over-enthusiastically playing ping pong and to the delight of his audience (mostly girls), speaking loudly in a really lame Chinese accent. Very silly and politically incorrect, but funny goes a long way with me, and he made me snorty-laugh.

RUSS

All of a sudden, this gorgeous young woman walks in and my world just stopped. I hadn't been dating for almost a year, but I saw her, and my mouth just dropped. I couldn't speak. It was like that old saying, "You'll know that she's the one when you see her." That's immediately how I felt when I saw Tori Timm.

TORI

As the evening session started, I was surprised to see him leading the singing. I thought, "Wow, that came out of *him*? That sounds like a full-blown, grown-up voice and it's coming out of this goofy guy running around entertaining everybody." Afterwards, he walked right up to me and started talking; we ended up staying up really late, just getting to know each other. I definitely wasn't all Bambi-eyed infatuated with him right away, but I thought he was really interesting and kind. We talked about deep subjects and told funny stories. He even sang me a song at one point, as guys with guitars often do. It all felt natural and easy.

It's worth mentioning that I was dating the quarterback of the high school at the time and had been for about two years. We were right in the middle of breaking-up, so I was in the throes of teenage heartbreak, from my teeth to my toenails. I was convinced life was not going to go on. And I was not remotely looking to date anybody, much less fall in love.

Before the weekend was over, Russ got my phone number and he started calling me. It worked out well because my break-up angst was causing a lot of sleepless nights. He would call and just start shooting the breeze, telling me crazy stories about growing up with his brothers, making me laugh. He kept it light, but it also felt warm and safe. I'd wake up in the morning with the phone receiver still in my hand, having had fallen asleep to him talking. He did that every night for weeks.

Mama June

All the time that Russ lived with us, he didn't date much. His whole life was music, so his love life was pretty nonexistent. If the kids dated, it would always be a group date. We had a bible study at my house and there were all kinds of teenagers coming, so there were always girls around.

But he never brought one home, even though they were all crazy about him.

When he brought Tori home, I knew something different was going on because she was, first of all, different from the little Pentecostal girls that he had dated before. She was vivacious and funny, alive and beautiful. And he was totally smitten with her. Old-fashioned word, but "smitten" is the word. He absolutely adored her, and so did we.

She has been one of the beautiful blessings that came along with Russ, as well as my two grandchildren. I didn't know that I was going to get all that when I brought that boy home from school. But Russ chose well. Tori is a beautiful, intelligent, and sensitive woman. And she has been not only the love of his life, but also an asset to his career.

After the QB and I finally called it quits, I had no desire to jump back into the dating pool. It had been an intense relationship, and my heart needed to heal. Russ, the sly one, suggested, "My band plays concerts in churches and coffee houses on the weekends. Why don't you come and hang out with us, because then if someone tries to ask you out you can say that you already have plans?"

So began my first foray into traveling on the road with a bunch of music guys. All I remember from these early days is being crammed in the backseat of a lot of cars with guys who would take their shoes off. And the smell. Bobby Mason had the stinkiest feet in life. We ate gas station pizza late at night and sang along with the radio as loud as we could. For someone who ended up spending a substantial portion of her life traveling the world on a bus with a band, those coffee houses and stinky feet were a good training ground.

More than anything it was fun, effortless, and light. I never felt like Russ was asking for anything more. Every once in a while, Russ would say something like "I love being around you." It was very endearing, not pushy. He presented himself as a strong, solid adult, even at twenty years old. He'd seen more of the world than I had, he'd been to college and lived on his own. I didn't want things to get romantic because I didn't want to ruin what I thought, if nothing else, was going to be a deep friendship that would last a long time.

After this went on for about six months, Russ was bringing me home one night. My head was leaned back, eyes closed because it was so late after a concert somewhere. Russ said something funny, and I laughed and blurted out, "I just love you." And all I could think was, *Way to go, Tori, you just blew it*. It had been so easy and uncomplicated up to that point. This could change everything. I walked inside, closed the door, leaned up against it and said, "Well, that was really stupid." I felt horrible. The next time Russ called he acted as if it didn't even happen. But we both knew it did.

Even though Russ made me feel completely safe and protected, I was still nervous about actually falling in love with him. I didn't want to get hurt again. After I got over being horrified at myself for actually saying "I love you" out loud, I slowly started growing into the realization that, "Yeah, I really do." I finally relaxed and just let our relationship start evolving naturally, at its own pace. We grew closer and closer, to the point that I couldn't imagine my life without him. We got engaged sometime during that next year and were married a year after that.

RUSS

After being with Tori on that first retreat weekend, I lost my appetite for four days. I seriously couldn't even eat, I just knew in my heart she was the one. It felt right. When my appetite came back, I was already in love. Of course, I had been praying for her for years. *"Jesus, I know she's coming. I know she's going to be here. Help me be patient."* Mama June used to say to me, "I hope you find that spark that will hold you to that person for the rest of your life." With Tori, I felt that spark. It was like a soul connection.

Honestly, I didn't even know what love was, coming out of a home where love was withheld unless you did everything right, *then* you might get it. But if you did something that Mom and Dad didn't approve of, the love would be pulled away. And you would feel so alone. I didn't want to use my emotions to try to manipulate her, like I had learned growing up. I certainly didn't want to use my anger to try to control her. The last thing I wanted to do was turn into my father.

These first days with Tori were the first time that I began to use words to express how I felt, trying not to hide behind my emotions or feelings. And I love how she would use her words to tell me what she needed, what she wanted in a relationship.

Certainly, there was physical attraction. There was a lot about Tori to be physically attracted to, but it was more than that. Like the parable in the Bible, I felt that Tori was the treasure I had found in the field. This was what I have been looking for.

I tried so hard to not get too physical with her. Being raised Pentecostal, I knew I'd go straight to hell.

Tori: *He was always a very passionate guy. Those little Pentecostal boys will surprise you. I thought,* Whoa, there's a lot of pent-up energy in there! Who knew? *But you were very much a gentleman...ish.*

Russ: *Well, it was on purpose. I wanted it to be different with you. Because with other girls I had dated, so much of it was just, uh, hormones.*

Tori: *Do you want to mention any names?*

Russ: *Better not.*

She filled a hole inside me that I didn't even know was there. There was this longing, this emptiness, that I had been carrying around inside of me. It was like I finally had a purpose. I had somebody to move forward with, plan a life with. Tori was solid ground.

* * * * *

After we had been dating a while, the Sounds of Joy went to California for some concerts and were coming back through Arizona. We were exploring a neat Native American arts and crafts shop and I saw this little promise ring with a tiny diamond in it. I think it was thirty dollars, which was huge back then. Maybe not huge, but big enough that I second guessed my idea. I loved her, and I just wanted her to know.

When we got home, I told Tori, "I saw this ring at this shop in Arizona. I really liked it, and I want you to have it." She smiled and admired it, thanked me and put it on. But two weeks later I went to her house and her older sister Liz came walking out with that ring on her hand.

Tori: *Okay, she was just borrowing it for the evening. She had a date and was accessorizing.*

Russ: *I thought, "So apparently Tori didn't know this was a promise ring?"*

Tori: *Well, you weren't very clear. So it was like Rachel and Leah. The wrong sister.*

Russ: *It really hurt my feelings. I explained to Tori that it wasn't intended to just be a souvenir, it had a lot of meaning behind it. She was very embarrassed and apologized over and over.*

Tori: *And Liz never wore it again, just so you know. But it really did go with her outfit.*

I never pressured Tori, but I wanted her to know how I felt about her. I was always very cautious about, "Am I pushing too hard?" I just wanted her to turn to me, and she did, she started turning toward me which made me incredibly happy. When I gave her that ring, it was one of the first times I asked for something that was important to me. And she heard me.

I always tried to be there for her. Whenever she couldn't go to sleep, we'd talk until she fell asleep. When other people heard about this, they'd say, "What a nice thing to do. What a great youth leader to reach out like that, giving up sleep so you could encourage this girl and continue leading her to the Lord." They'd say that because compared to the way I grew up as a radical Pentecostal, Tori was barely a Christian! Little did I know.

THREE

LEAVING ARKANSAS

There was an evangelist from Fort Worth named Jerry Savelle who would come to Arkansas and hold three-day revivals in hotel ballrooms and churches. When he was in my area he would ask me to sing for the crowd before he preached. After a few times doing this together, he asked me, "Russ, would you consider coming to work with me? I'd love to have you sing and lead worship in my meetings, and I could use some help running things on the road." Of course, I couldn't help but think this was an awesome opportunity I was being offered. Jerry was an incredible teacher of the Word. And I would love to learn from him. But it was going to be hard to walk away from the band, and I hated to think about being that far away from Tori. And Bud and June.

You don't know how many times I've heard, "Get a real job. This singing thing won't pay the bills." I knew I was called to something, and I knew music was a part of it. I never thought in a million years that it would happen like it eventually did. Perhaps a part of my decision to go work with Jerry was simply being tired of arguing with people. I was hoping Jerry's offer of a weekly paycheck to sing would shut up the naysayers.

Tori was very supportive of my decision, and Bud and June helped me buy a little green Pinto. I packed up two boxes and my guitar and headed to Fort Worth. Once I got outside of the city limits, I stopped, got out of my car, turned around and yelled, "Hey, Hot Springs, one day I'll come back to this town and everybody will know my name!" I stood there for a few minutes with tears rolling down my face. Then got back into my car and continued on my trek. I was going to be somebody. I had something to prove.

I had two of the best years of my life with Jerry Savelle. Every weekend I led worship, then he would preach. When our Friday night meetings were over, I'd take Jerry to where he was staying, then I'd go back, straighten everything up, and turn everything off. Then I would take the cassette of that night's sermon back to my room and make fifty copies to have available for the next day's product table. I'd repeat that for the morning session, then the evening session again.

It's as if Jerry recognized a young man who needed to be fathered. He certainly stepped into that role and displayed tremendous integrity as a man of faith. Sitting under Jerry's teaching for those years was life-changing. It was so unlike the doctrine I grew up in, with its ramrod rules and wild emotionalism. This was real, solid teaching, practical Christianity. And I soaked it up.

While I was in Fort Worth, Tori and I would talk constantly on the phone. Our long-distance bills were astronomical, but we were building our relationship even across the miles. And then I'd come back to Arkansas as often as I could during the week. I wanted to see Tori, Bud, and June. But mostly Tori.

One weekend trip home, she and I paid a visit to West Mountain in Hot Springs, a place with a beautiful view where people would park and talk. Aw, who am I kidding? We went there to make out.

In the middle of our "talking," I took a breather, looked her in the eyes, and said, "Will you marry me?"

TORI

Let me jump in here. I said yes, of course, or we wouldn't be here right now. But I will tell you the truth. In my mind, I felt *young*. You always feel like you know more than you do when you're twenty, so I didn't feel immature, but I felt inexperienced. Even though I knew we weren't going to do anything sudden, the first fleeting thought that came into my head when Russ asked me—and I'm not even kidding—was, "Well, maybe this will be my *first* marriage."

I'm not exactly sure where that thought even came from. My parents stayed together; they were married seventy-two years when they died. All of my five brothers and sisters were married at the time. So, it wasn't like I'd never been around relationships that go the distance. But even though I knew I wanted to marry him, it just felt like we came from two very different places. Russ had been out on his own for years and was impatient to get his life and career rolling. I was excited about the future, but I also had deep solid roots that connected me to my family. He was attentive, funny, and wise, but could also be restless, moody, and withdrawn. He was definitely more "spiritual-acting" than I was. I loved God, but I had a mouth on me, too! It's almost as if there was a distant warning bell—even though everything felt and looked good, there was some part of the rock that we were planning to build our lives on that felt more like tectonic plates that might do some serious shifting over time. But in my twenty-year-old wisdom, I decided to ignore those niggling little doubts. I knew Russ was crazy about me, so surely he'd try extra hard to make things work. I figured that if anyone was gonna screw up this marriage, it would probably be me.

When I look back and see how our life has gone, it's funny. I secretly thought when we got married that Russ's feelings for me were deeper and more intense than the ones I had for him. The irony is that years later, by the time things got really bad between us, my love for him had grown so strong that I was the one who held on tighter, fought harder, and refused to give up. Until I finally had to.

RUSS

Even though Tori and I already agreed that we'd get married, there was still one person I needed to talk to about our decision. This was a time when it was normal for the guy to ask his girlfriend's dad for permission to marry her. I was so nervous because on paper, I didn't necessarily look like I was a very safe bet. Especially since Don, Tori's dad, was a very practical man. He managed furniture stores, raised six kids, and was a steady provider with everything figured out right down to the penny. I was convinced he was going to see me as a flighty musician-type without any financial security. When we met, I said to him, "I promise that I will take care of Tori to the best of my ability and be the kind of husband that you would be proud of."

I was so relieved when he kindly gave us his blessing.

Tori had been working at a school with special needs children and was home with the flu. I went to see her on one of my weekend trips home. She was sitting up in bed, trying not to throw up. That's when I pulled out the ring I got from Service Merchandise and made it official.

We were engaged for a full year, going back and forth on the phone and in person when we could. Everything was in place—the wedding date was set, the invitations were ordered. We had an apartment service looking for apartments down in Fort Worth and everything was geared towards us getting married, honeymooning in Jamaica, and moving to Texas. And then the phone call came.

"Is this Russ Taff?" the voice on the other end asked.

"Yes, sir."

"This is Joe Moscheo. I manage The Imperials and heard you sing when we were in Hot Springs a couple of years ago."

Did they want to come back and do another concert? I started to tell him how, at this time, I wasn't in a place to pay to bring them back.

"No, I'm not calling about another concert. We have an opening in our group and I wanted to see if you'd consider coming to Nashville to audition?"

I felt my knees start shaking. I was so shocked that he would call me. He told me that Sherman Andrus and Terry Blackwood were leaving the group and they were looking for replacements.

"Something tells me you'd have a pretty good shot, if you did," he added. I didn't know what to make of that last comment. But I thought, *why not?* Nothing ventured, nothing gained, right?

We set a date, and I trekked up to Nashville. Me and my trusty Pinto. That afternoon I sang with the group; Jim Murray, Armond Morales, and Dave Will. And that evening they offered me the position.

This dream job came at a time when I was the happiest I had ever been in my life. Because of working with Jerry, I was growing in in my faith and I was starting to get a glimpse of a Jesus that was very different than the one I grew up hearing about in Eastside Tabernacle. Jerry was confident and motivated, which was a great example for me to be around.

I was successfully blocking out most of the negative voices in my head I had listened to while growing up, thinking the best way to deal with them was to just act like they weren't even there. Maybe it wasn't as bad as I remembered. Maybe if I just kept moving forward, focused on building a career and making a life with Tori, the horrible memories of being shamed and beaten would just fade away with time. Unfortunately, those insecurities that I always managed to bring into every situation kept me from fully trusting the good things that were happening in my life. Still, I did feel some version of peace—even if it was only on the surface and could sense a strong undertow not too far below. But peace on the surface was more than I had ever known. I was grateful.

The thing that impressed me so much about Jerry Savelle is that even though he could have talked me out of taking this new job, he didn't. Everything in me wanted to say yes immediately to The Imperials. *The Imperials!* But I still wasn't completely sure of my own ability to make such a huge decision.

"Jerry, if you want me to stay, I will." I knew he was relying on me to help him with the meetings on the weekends, then office work during the week.

I'll never forget what Jerry said because it could've gone either way. He said, "If you would have asked me this six months ago, I would have thought maybe you're not ready… but you're exactly where you need to be."

He continued, "Russ, this would be like if Oral Roberts called me up and said he wanted me to help him in his ministry." Which is funny because later that did happen, and Jerry went to Tulsa and worked with Oral for a long time. "Russ, I want you to pray about it. Whatever you decide, I'm going to consider it the wisdom of God. And I'll support you in it."

That really impressed me and helped give me the confidence to leave my safe little Fort Worth life. His encouragement and vote of confidence had such a profound effect on me that I've always tried to pass that on to others. It's the responsibility of ministries to birth other ministries, and Jerry certainly did that with me. It's been over forty years since that man sent me out into the world with his blessing, and I've never forgotten it.

After two weeks I accepted The Imperials' offer and we were off to Nashville, Tennessee.

TORI

Let's not forget that we had all the wedding invitations ordered from New York ready to send out, the date set, and my dream honeymoon to Jamaica planned. And suddenly Russ is jumping on a bus with The Imperials, fulfilling concert obligations that had been booked months and months before, including one on the exact date of our wedding. *The best laid plans...*

My mom came up with the brilliant idea of having a little card printed that we stuck in the envelope of my fancy invitations that said the wedding date has been changed. October 17th was the day we had planned on getting married and, wouldn't you know it, the only date that Russ would be available in the entire month of October was

Halloween. My mother thought that was the funniest thing ever. She laughed, "You ought to have the bridesmaids carry jack-o'-lanterns!" Thank you, Imperials.

But nobody ever forgets our anniversary.

RUSS

When the singer I was replacing, Sherman Andrus, heard that I had been hired, he decided to leave the group early. Armond Morales, the bass singer and co-owner of the group with tenor Jim Murray, called and said, "You better come on, because he's going to leave early. And I want you to see a couple concerts before he leaves."

That's when Tori and I went up to Nashville, stayed at her brother Matt's house, and looked for an apartment. Then three weeks before the wedding I was on the bus and we were off. I was twenty-two years old and I've been riding buses ever since.

The night before the wedding, The Imperials drove all night and then the bus would drop me off at an airport to make my 8:00 a.m. flight back into Hot Springs for our Halloween wedding. I couldn't sleep all night with the guys joking around with me, saying, "I just don't know if we're going to make it in time." I was really worried. "What would I say to Tori if I missed my flight?" So, I sat in the front seat by the driver all night long, thinking maybe I could somehow will the bus to get there on time.

On Sunday morning, October 31, 1976, the Hot Springs courthouse opened up for us to get our wedding license. My dad, who had come in from California with mom and Earl, co-officiated the small ceremony with the elderly pastor of my parent's church. Words can't describe how I felt when I saw Tori in her dress.

It was a beautiful ceremony. It was also hilarious. My dad Pentecostal-preached his way through our vows at the top of his lungs, which caused a lot of startled looks among the congregation. And then at the end, the ninety-something-year-old pastor, who looked like he might not live long enough to finish the wedding, wheezed out a barely audible benediction. Tori and I caught each other's eye and tried really hard not to crack up, but my shoulders were shaking and her bridal bouquet was jiggling. God absolutely knew what I needed when this high school cheerleader walked into my life.

The next day, Tori and I jumped in the Pinto with a box full of wedding presents and drove to Nashville. We jumped on the bus with the guys and head to the West Coast.

Tori: *Hold on, you just skipped over the honeymoon.*

Russ: *Sorry. Yes. Tori's father's boss had a beautiful condo on a lake in Hot Springs. He let us have it for our wedding night. We were opening gifts after the wedding, and honestly, we were pretty well undressed because we had been making out.*

Tori: *"Making out?" We were married, for crying out loud.*

Russ: *Well, I'm trying to keep this...*

Tori: *PG?*

Russ: *Christian, yes.*

Tori: *Oh please, like Christians don't…? Anyway, we had just gotten out of the bathtub, and we were sitting there, butt naked on the living room floor opening our wedding presents. And getting money that was now* not *going to go towards a Jamaican honeymoon. And then what happened, Russ?*

Russ: *Well, the doorbell rang, and we heard,* trick or treat! *So, we dove for the lights and hit the deck, trying to get out of sight.*

Tori: *We did a G. I. Joe crawl across the floor, while kids dressed up like ghosts and Disney princesses peered in through the glass door.*

Russ: *It went on for nearly two hours. Even after we turned the lights off, still,* trick or treat! *We were laughing so hard.*

Tori: *I said, "Maybe we should we give them wedding presents? I don't think we're going to need this blender, here kid."*

Russ: *Oh, it was funny.*

Tori: *Yeah, that was memorable.*

From the beginning, Tori went on the road with us, sharing a bunk with me—which is a bit like two people sleeping in a coffin. We would need to have a meeting if one of us wanted to turn over. It's probably something only newlywed crazy-in-love young people would ever consider a fun way to start married life, but we sure did. Tori loved to travel and every time we'd hit a new town, she'd take off to experience that city. She was so cheerful and enthusiastic. Wherever she was, she loved it. Watching her, I began to learn how to do that a little bit. Because of the way I grew up, I learned to live turned inward, constantly trying to protect myself, justifiably not wanting to be hurt any more. I would let in very few people because experience taught me it's not safe to do that. But Tori lived life wide open.

TORI

Turns out quartet guys are traditionally a little weird about having wives on the bus, but The Imperials were very sweet and gracious to me. Their wives would go on the road occasionally, but they all had kids at home, so we were in very different places in our lives. I kind of became the group's mascot. I didn't go on every trip, but they were gone some three-hundred-plus days a year, so it was either go with them or never see Russ. I thought it was all so exciting. I didn't have enough sense to know I should not enjoy sleeping under a snoring drummer. I was more thinking, *Yippee! I've never been to the West Coast. Let's go.* It was the beginning of our great adventure.

Oh, and they didn't have a bathroom on the bus. The guys had a funnel contraption they'd use, but since I wasn't anatomically equipped for that, if I had to go, the driver had to find a truck stop and stop the whole dang bus. In my effort to not be any trouble, I developed the bladder of a camel. I believe I still hold The Imperials' bus record, which is sixteen and a half hours without having to pull over.

Travel was new, having our own apartment was new, having a husband was new. We were like Hansel and Gretel in the woods, finding our way through it all together. It was always a partnership. And from the beginning, even though he was the guy on stage, I never felt like I was in Russ' shadow. I was the youngest of six in my family, so I became the show-off at an early age. I always had plenty to bring to the party.

Everything we were experiencing for the first time we were experiencing together. I'd never been on a bus and had the air conditioning go out in the middle of the Mojave Desert before. I'd never seen Los Angeles before. I'd never followed the Pacific Coast Highway all the way to Oregon before. It was all new and fun and wonderful, and it solidified the friendship part of our marriage because we were together night and day. And then we'd come home to Nashville and be together night and day in between trips.

I didn't always go with Russ on the road. Sometimes I liked being home alone, at least for a while. But there were times when I was in our little Nashville apartment and would be so homesick for my big noisy family in Arkansas that I'd just sit on my 1970s earth-toned loveseat eating BBQ potato chips, crying until I couldn't see straight. Russ was so understanding when he'd call me from the road and could tell I was blue.

We had only been married a few months, and Russ was home for a couple of days. He was down in the kitchen, and when he came up the stairs to our room, he could see that I was teary. He said, "What's wrong?"

I said, "I just think I'm a little lonesome for home."

Right then, he put one hundred dollars—which was a lot of money to us—in a drawer and said, "I know you've never been away from your family before, so we're going to keep this money right here and any time you need to go see them, you can use it to buy a plane ticket home." This meant so much to me. My family is my touchstone, my safe place, and so much a part of who I am. And I absolutely used that money a couple of times.

FOUR

FAMILIAR GROUND

The Imperials released their first record in 1964. Formed by long-time Statesmen Quartet member, Jake Hess, the group was a Southern Gospel supergroup of sorts, with different members coming from other popular groups. They would go on to become pioneers in the growing Contemporary Christian music genre, loosening their grips on their Southern gospel roots, and borrowing more from pop and rock, relying on faith-based lyrics to convey the message. They sang backup with Elvis in Vegas, were regulars on *The Jimmy Dean Show*, and won all kinds of awards. They were big time.

When I joined The Imperials, they were just starting to make the transition from a gospel quartet to a Contemporary Christian group. My vocal style fit the bill for the direction they wanted to go. For me, it was quite the transition going from singing with Jerry in Holiday Inn ballrooms that would hold two hundred people, to my first date with The Imperials at Ball State University where there were six thousand. I was so overwhelmed when I walked out on stage and it was just a sea of people looking at us.

From the beginning, I was very cautious about being compared to Sherman Andrus, the singer who I replaced. People really loved him. The group had about five or six big songs that he sang lead on, and I asked if I could not sing lead on those tunes, so Dave and Jim took a lot of those leads. For the first year or so I just sang harmonies. The only song I would sing lead on was "He Looked Beyond My Faults." Singing that great Dottie Rambo song allowed me to create my own sound. Armond and Jim were very gracious through those early days to let me experiment.

Jim Murray, Tenor for The Imperials

Russ joining our group came at a very pivotal time for The Imperials. Here comes this guy with this incredible voice— and he's a good songwriter. If we had been smarter we would've jumped on all of Russ' songs. He brought this rough, edgy, soulful sound that we really had not had. The first time we sang with him, it fit like a glove. He was a big influence in changing our direction to a more contemporary style than southern gospel.

I was so excited to be in The Imperials, and when they needed a guitar player, I recommended my old friend James Hollihan. They hired him immediately, so James and his bride Sis moved to Nashville, too. Tori and I didn't have a lot of expenses, so money wasn't a big issue. I did figure out early on that the owners of the group, Armond and Jim, wanted to keep a cap on salaries. They had built and maintained this group for years and they were not interested in profit sharing.

I had always dreamed of making my own record. I told Armond the first year I was there, "I'm not going anywhere, but at some point, I would love to have the opportunity to write some songs and do a solo record." I was so hungry to learn how to take a song, build it, and go into the studio and create. That was a huge passion of mine. And I was also thinking about mine and Tori's future and how I could help build our family by being more financially stable. Having my own product to sell would be a good start. Armond and Jim didn't flat-out say no, but they weren't exactly enthusiastic.

Another time, I asked if I could be paid per night instead of having a weekly salary. At our peak, when we were selling out huge venues, our records were flying off the shelves and radio was playing hit after hit, I was bringing home 425 dollars a week. About three years in, I thought if I could maybe get paid per concert instead of a flat salary, it would make more sense for me financially. Not anything big, just 150 dollars a night. And then maybe I could also start booking some small solo church dates for additional income. These two ideas were shut down pretty quickly. Armond said, "I have a list of names as long as my arm of singers who are ready to replace you in a heartbeat." He wasn't being a jerk, it was just that old-school quartet style of management. I saw then that I was not going to be able to grow as an artist or develop a career here. Those desires had to be put on hold. I was simply the hired singer, and I needed to learn to do what I was told.

After a while, things began to get to the point that it wasn't a good place for me. They wanted to keep me humble and not let my head get too big, so I wouldn't think about leaving the group. If this all sounds too familiar to you, imagine what ghosts from the past these comments rustled up for me. It was like I was back in my house in California, trying to earn approval and show I was worth something.

* * * * *

Contemporary music like ours was making big moves in the Christian marketplace. Because of this, our producers Chris Christian, Brown Bannister, Michael Omartian, and Buddy Huey from Word Records, kept throwing more and more solos my way because I had the most contemporary sounding voice. This created conflict between Jim and myself.

Jim is an incredibly talented Irish tenor who would absolutely blow everybody away when he performed. But after I joined the group and we began to move towards a more contemporary sound, the albums didn't feature him as often as before. And he did not like it very much.

We were making our first record together, *Sail On*, and our producer Chris started giving me more and more solos. I met with Armond and Jim and said, "Guys, this is a quartet and maybe we should spread out the leads some to where I'm not singing this block of songs," but they didn't approach Chris. It seemed like every record we did I was getting more and more solos. There was increasing tension in the group, but no one knew quite what to do about it. They weren't happy about the fact that I was being featured more, but they couldn't argue with the success the group was having. When we headed out for our West Coast run, I remember thinking, "How am I going to spend five weeks on a bus with someone that doesn't like me very much?"

We were at Tori's mom's house for Thanksgiving, and we were all talking about this weird situation in which I had found myself. Her mom said, "Russ, you know how they used to purify precious stones? They would take the rough stone right out of the ground and put it in a vat of BBs. The vat would spin, shake, and tumble the stone around until it had knocked off all the jagged edges, so when the stone came out, it was clean, smooth, and pure. Do you think maybe the Holy Spirit's doing that to you?"

I did not want to hear that. At that time in my life, the only role I knew how to play was the victim. It felt like I was being treated unfairly, and I brooded about that. Resentment was growing on both sides.

One day when we were out on tour I was praying and listening to a sermon on cassette. The preacher said, "It's easy to love somebody who loves you. But can you reach out with the love of Christ to somebody who doesn't love you back?" That's when I purposed in my heart to walk in the love of God no matter what.

I had just spent two and a half years with Jerry Savelle, who was a caring, encouraging person; and then I went into a group where it wasn't like that anymore. It was a struggle, but it was also familiar. I knew how to live in that kind of environment because I'd spent my whole childhood living with jealousy.

The first thing I made myself do was to shut my mouth and not get sucked into arguments. When I felt anger rising, I didn't respond. I was so ready to leave, but I never could get a release in my spirit. I would pray, "God get me out of here." But the release never came. Eventually I got pretty good at faking it until I made it, and gradually something began to change in me. I come from a family of quitters—when it gets hard you quit. When you feel like you have been attacked unjustly—you quit. Through those years with The Imperials I learned not to quit. And I tried my best to walk every day in love no matter what. Just shut my mouth and love.

God used that situation to teach me how to be consistent, a man who honors his word. It didn't always come naturally, but I was determined to hang tough and stick to it.

We were performing in Lincoln, Nebraska just prior to our *Priority* record coming out. A situation happened that day that really frustrated me. I was tired. I was tired of the fight, tired of the struggle. A little voice that I believe was the Lord said to me, "I'm coming to hear you sing tonight." He said, "I love to hear you sing." And I just started crying. My real Dad was coming to hear me sing. It was a small crowd, maybe only a third full on a Tuesday night. The guys didn't know what to think because I went out there and sang like I was at Carnegie Hall. That thought has stayed with me all these years. Even now, when I'm getting ready to go out and sing, I think *He's coming tonight. And He loves to hear me sing.*

Sometime during that concert, Dave Will stepped up to sing a solo. I was standing with Jim on one side of me and Armond on the other. And out of nowhere Jim leaned over, put a hand on my shoulder and quietly said in my ear, "I love you, Russ." I was blindsided by that. It felt like a true peace offering. Not only did God change my attitude, but it seemed like it changed Jim's as well. I'm so thankful that over the years Jim and I have become good friends. But as soon as he said those words that Tuesday night in Lincoln, I immediately knew that was my release. I could leave the group. I passed the test. I did it. I walked in love with somebody that was not loveable at the time. And within five weeks I was gone. I left before *Priority* even came out.

TORI

I started noticing differences in Russ in the first year and a half of our marriage. Yes, everything was a whirlwind and I was having a lot of fun, but I hadn't lived with him before. Whenever you spend all your time with someone, you see parts of their personality you never noticed before. I first started noticing mood changes. Not big manic swings, but just slowly darkening moods—enough to raise my eyebrow from time to time.

Russ has no poker face. I could literally tell what was going on inside his head when he walked in the door. It was a bit like the little dust cloud in Peanuts, constantly following Pigpen around.

In the kind of Pentecostal religion he grew up, everything was fed by emotion. If you didn't feel emotion, it wasn't God. I knew Russ had an intense part of him—I liked that. When it's focused on you in a positive way, it's very powerful. But I started noticing that there would be times when he was just emotionally withdrawn. He wasn't volatile, but he would get irritated more than usual.

Even at his worst, he was never violent or threatening. It would just be dark. And there was an intense sorrow in him that I would instinctively feel. I would catch a glimpse of him and his whole face was just sad.

I could never figure out why he was so sad. I sure tried. Being young and full of myself, I assumed that if he was happy, it had something to do with me. And if he was sad, it must have something to do with me, too.

RUSS

I was very, very shy when I first started singing. Even with The Imperials, Tori would always say, "Open your eyes, open your eyes!" I was intimidated by so many things. Tori says I'm an introvert trapped in an extrovert's career. I agree.

Back in high school, I started seeing the part of me that didn't like to be at parties. Everybody else seemed to be so excited about events like senior prom, saying "It's going to be so great!" And for me, the prom was just a giant, loud room filled with too many people, and me sitting against the wall feeling extremely uncomfortable.

Even now, when I go to a party or gathering, I always try to find one person that I can have a real conversation with. Small talk does not interest me at all, but soul talk does. I want to talk about something that's important. Usually it ends up being about Jesus. Because when He brings you through so much, that's all you want to talk about. Swapping golf stories doesn't do it for me.

Being around a lot of people wears me out, but Tori is the exact opposite. She gets energized, like she's had a double espresso. She is completely comfortable right off the bat and can talk to anybody. She used to beg me to go to parties and it just sounded exhausting to me. "I'm just not up for it," I'd tell her. But we came up with a clever compromise—when we go to a group function we take two cars. After thirty minutes, I'm ready to go. And then she can stay as long as she wants. Works great.

TORI

"I'll see him in a corner of the room in this intense conversation with somebody and I'll think, *Oh, he's having a good time.*"

RUSS

Some of this social uneasiness is closely related to depression, which probably started around the age of seventeen or eighteen, even though I didn't have an official diagnosis until much later. I'm very familiar with the feeling of being under the weight of some kind of strange heaviness. And unfortunately, you can't just climb or pray your way out of it.

I would get extremely lonely and feel very isolated. It would eventually start lessening after a while. But then, without a lot of warning or rhyme or reason I'd go back down into it. And Tori wouldn't know what was going on, she simply saw me being real quiet and withdrawn. On the inside, I couldn't help but wonder if something was wrong with my brain, like, "do I have a tumor?"

Some relief came when I had a therapist diagnose me with classic clinical depression—an imbalance in my brain chemistry, and fortunately, treatable. They started me on a regimen of medications trying to find the right antidepressant for me. Now, there's a whole bunch of them out there. But sometimes it takes a few tries to get one that really works with the serotonin in your brain.

Dealing with depression can make it difficult to be around people, like Bill Gaither or my wife, who are always so up, so ready for whatever the day will bring. I used to envy that, wondering, "Why can't I have one year of my life that is free of all this?" As you can imagine, being a performer presented me with a huge challenge.

Right before I'd walk out on stage, I'd have to mentally change clothes, knowing there was an expectation that I act a certain way. It was never fake—I was being authentic when I was in front of a crowd. The music and the speaking would make those fears go away and I was just one with God, one with the audience. There were times where I could feel his presence in a room. But unlike the old days when we'd "shout it off," I had to learn how to funnel it. To funnel the anointing to needs in the room, the people who are hurting and don't know what to do.

What happens in concerts has always been very important to me, but it would wear me out. It became so important to be able to retreat when those two hours were over, to just be quiet for a bit and get recharged again. It's not an easy process.

It became even more challenging to me when I started winning awards and people started gravitating toward me for various reasons. Some people would literally follow me around. Some would just want to talk. Some would want to see if I could help them in their own music careers. This made me retreat even more.

I tell Tori that if I hadn't married her, I'd be a hermit somewhere. Just give me my guitar and I'll be off on a mountain someplace far away. I'd be like David, just sitting around with a bunch of sheep, singing songs to God all day long. Obviously, that hasn't been my story.

Because my life has been so public, I had to learn how to build a perimeter around my heart and my life that I could live within. It's a way to protect myself so people don't come all the way in. I'm thankful that I can walk into a room now and control it. I don't have to give in to my fear, my anxiety, or my need to be a people pleaser. I don't have to give all of myself away to everybody, which is what was so exhausting.

It helped me to work the record table after the shows, being out in the lobby and meeting people. I find I can tell a person a part of my story or a few lines that might encourage them—that part is good. I see the benefit in being engaged with people, even if it's not me laying all my guts out on the table. I've found a place that feels natural to me, and it doesn't feel hypocritical. I'm comfortable in my own skin and what I'm doing, but now I control the scenario and it doesn't control me. I wish I would've learned this a long time ago.

I probably wouldn't have much of a career if it wasn't for Tori and her ability to talk to people and win them over so easily. We could go to a party, and I would point her toward certain people saying, "That guy is from Word Records, would you go introduce yourself to him?" So many times, people fell in love with her before they started liking me because she's just so genuinely interested in them. It was so comfortable for her.

TORI

If you put me up on a stage with a microphone in front of a crowd of people, my knees will shake, and I'll be no good to anybody. But offstage? I'm the baby of the family, the one who had to try harder to get noticed—I know how to work the room at a party. At our best, our two different personalities complement each other and it's seamless.

RUSS

It took us a while to understand this process of emptying and needing to recharge. I would come off the road and Tori would say, "You gave yourself away to all those people at your concerts, and now you have nothing left over for us?" I would certainly try. But we both began to discover the importance of my need to decompress after all the socializing. Now when I come home, she'll say hello, hug and kiss me, and then she lets me sit on the couch, watch something mindless on TV, and hibernate. Then in twenty-four hours, I'm ready to go.

TORI

It's a bit like, "So when is Russ coming home?" And I'll say, "Well, physically he'll be here Tuesday, but by about

Wednesday afternoon, he'll actually be home." At best it's a healthy give and take. At worst, it's like, "Hey Russ, remember me?"

RUSS

My hiding and being emotionally unavailable couldn't all be blamed on my shyness, or even my depression. I had big secrets that I couldn't tell anyone for fear of losing everything that was important to me. What I couldn't see was that I was sabotaging the very things I loved, making it easier and easier to lose what I held most dear.

Like Tori.

I WANT TO CHANGE

Lord, You know my past
Like clay the pains of life
Have molded me
The years have brought
So many things
From examples I could see
Some good
Some bad
They're all a part of me
But I see my selfish motives
And my inconsistencies
And block upon block
The wall was built complete
Oh, please, come
And break the wall down
And show this captive heart
How to be free

I STILL BELIEVE

I want to be like You
I want to change
And not be trapped in the patterns
My life has set for me
I want to be like You
Please help me change
Into what I was meant to be
Until all I can clearly see
Is the loving reflection
Of You in me

Teach me to forgive
Letting go of hurts I hide behind
Facing all of the things in me
I've buried deep inside
As Your healing love
Brings all of them to light
Let my life be an example
Of what true life can be
When it's given like a gift
To those who need
Oh, please, come
And take control of
This yielded, willing soul
And live through me

(lyrics by Russ & Tori Taff)

Bart Millard, MercyMe

I grew up in a way similar to Russ. I was raised in a legalistic church where Christ is enough, but here are ten more things you can do just to make sure. I became the overachiever. The reason I started the band was because I was trying to be Super Christian—I wanted God to notice me, be pleased with me, and like me better than most people. Then about five years ago, I hit a wall and didn't want to do the MercyMe thing anymore. I realized I can't be perfect enough; the whole religiosity of it got to me. Kingdom work was becoming the villain that took Daddy away from home for my kids.

I started talking to Russ about this. He said, "Man, I've been there a million times." Between Russ and some of my friends, I started learning more about grace. That regardless of anything I do, Christ can't love me anymore than he already does right now. Russ would say, "If it wasn't for grace, I wouldn't be breathing."

Russ became a great cheerleader for me saying, "This message of grace is spot on. Don't stop." I'd tell him that some of the gatekeepers of older churches say that I've lost my mind and that we don't care about sin, that it's too much grace. Russ would say, "Don't listen to them." I don't know if he realizes how instrumental he's been in keeping us on the path that we're on now, to where we love making music more than ever before.

Russ has this amazing gift of looking at someone, regardless of the things they've done, and still seeing them as a brother and sister in Christ with no condemnation. That's probably because of what he went through. That's why I always think suffering is a gift because it's hard to really imagine what grace is without it, and Russ knows what grace is...that's for sure.

FIVE

SPINNING THE BOTTLE

I couldn't help but be grateful for how being with The Imperials put me in front of thousands of people. They gave me so many great opportunities. Yeah, I could be upset that I didn't feel like I was treated right, but on the other hand, they literally brought me to the party and to the attention of so many record labels. I'm glad I didn't quit.

There was something really wonderful about the years that the four of us were together making music in LA with the greatest players of the time. We won three Grammys while I was there. Those were such exciting times. The record company would get a limo and take us to the Shrine Auditorium for the ceremony. I walked in wearing a tux with gorgeous Tori on my arm, and there was Bruce Springsteen and Michael Jackson. Gospel music is sort of the redheaded stepchild of the music industry, but I was proud of the music we were making. One year we even had the opportunity to sing on the show. Being on national television was not only a big deal for us, but for the record company, Christian music fans, and all our families and friends. I loved thinking about Bud and June watching us in Arkansas.

While were singing "Sail On" I looked down the front row and there was Sting and James Taylor—everyone that I was listening to. I couldn't look at them for fear of completely forgetting my words. I don't know how many millions of people saw us. And then there are parties afterward. Everyone would come together and toast you. It was such a thrill.

But there is so much that people didn't see. Like the fact that since I was the youngest in the group, I had to drive from 1:00 a.m. to 7:00 a.m. I'd sleep during the day, sing at night, and then drive until the morning. For a lot of the time, I was just numb. I didn't really know how to handle the attention I was receiving from thousands of fans clapping and telling me how wonderful I was. I had created a persona of the happy, confident guy, which is what I thought people wanted to see, and I worked hard to keep it up. But behind it was a prisoner of war who was starving to death. People would look at the image and think it all must be so wonderful.

I kept trying to act like all the childhood trauma and covert incest didn't happen. But it shaped who I had become. It deformed my spirit. I had no idea what normal was. The only normal I knew was chaos.

I would drive all night and listen to Black Gospel and old Southern Gospel quartet, but nothing would ever get down to where the pain was. Nothing could feed this profound hunger in me. I was also dealing with hardcore depression, so even while people are saying "Boy, he's the luckiest guy in the world," my heart was dying. I didn't know what to do with all this rage and pain.

All the voices I heard in my childhood held me captive. I could win a Grammy, go back to my fancy hotel, and after thirty minutes I'd feel worthless again. Remember how I learned as a kid to never tell anybody what's going on in the family? I was doing that again as an adult. I was hiding, even from Tori. I showed her the image. She never knew how deeply broken I was and how I so desperately needed to be healed. Alone, I'd cry out in my prayers, "Somebody help me, somebody help me. God help me…" I started to say hateful, critical things to myself because that's what I was taught.

HEALING TOUCH

I stare at the door
Trapped in a dream
Held like a captive
By what people see on the outside
They don't really know
And even with You
I deny what is real
The loving truth is a painful touch
When guilt is all you feel
I want to run away
You've got to help me stay

Your healing touch
To know Your love
Just to feel Your strength in me again
The rivers are deep
Where they're flowing
They're rolling through me
I want to be free

Shades of truth
Locked up in lies

Days run into days
When I open my eyes
See how far it's gone
Where do things go wrong
Choices were made
Dreams were pushed aside
Not so much a conscious thought
But resignation
A siege of the heart
But there's a part that calls to You

Bring me healing
I've got to know Your love again
I've grown weak
Let Your strength be mine again
The rivers are deep
Where they're flowing
They're rolling through me
You're the only one
Who can save me from myself

If I can make it today
There's hope for me tomorrow
I can't make it alone
Just not that strong

(lyrics Russ & Tori Taff, and James Hollihan)

I finally was able to find a bit of relief in a way that shocked me. Tori and I were visiting her brother Joel, a symphony oboist, and sister-in-law Kri, a dancer with American Ballet Theatre in New York. They were incredibly talented, fascinating people and loved showing off their city to us. New York was a whole different world, and we loved it. Tori dragged me to every museum and gallery she could find, and we splurged on tickets to Broadway shows and the ballet.

It was July in Greenwich Village, so it was hot. All the Cokes were gone from the fridge, but there was beer in there. In Nashville Christian circles, casual social drinking was not a big deal. But I never really liked the taste of alcohol, so I never drank myself. That day I didn't think too hard about it— my main priority was to cool down. I popped that beer open and started drinking it like a Coke. All of a sudden, I started feeling something. It's like there was always a constant static in my brain, and it kind of settled down. So, I had another. And another. Then all the pain went away. All the voices went away. For the first time in my life, my brain was quiet. I distinctly remember thinking, *this is a miracle. I can live this way. This must be how normal people feel all the time!*

I immediately, and instinctively, hid this from Tori. The very next night we had tickets to see *Joseph and the Amazing Technicolor Dreamcoat* on Broadway. I noticed there was a bar in the lobby, so after we found our seats, I excused myself to "go to the bathroom." I went straight to the bar and ordered the only cocktail I could think of, which was a Bloody Mary. Didn't even know what was in it, but I quickly downed two of them then went back to join Tori. At intermission, I excused myself again and drank a third one. I don't remember much of the subway ride back to Joel and Kri's apartment. Tori was happily reviewing the play, and I just sat really still to keep my head from spinning.

I never became a partier. I hardly ever drank anything around anybody. I simply craved the way it made me feel. I know it sounds bizarre, but I literally thanked Jesus for this "miracle drug" that I had found. It softened the edges, life didn't feel so hopeless. The thought of turning into my dad never really crossed my mind because of course that would never happen. I had finally found some peace. But I also started hiding, right from the get go. I knew better than to try to share my enthusiasm for what alcohol was doing for me with Tori.

I was sucked in so fast.

But after a relatively short amount of time, it turned on me. I didn't feel the euphoria anymore. The drinking began to increase the pain because there was so much guilt. Not to mention, the brilliant decision to pour a depressant down the throat of a depressed person. And the insanity of addiction is that, even when it wasn't magically working for me like it did at first, I just kept drinking. Eventually it got to where I had to have it every day just to get through the day. Then I'd start drinking earlier because of the hangovers. I felt sick all the time since I was literally putting poison in my body. The only way to not be sick is to drink more. Then that blessed numbness would come back.

That's when I started seriously hating myself. I hated what I had become. I hated that I couldn't quit. I would try to go a couple of weeks without drinking, but the draw was too strong. So, I kept hiding. I didn't talk about Jesus with the passion I used to in concerts, even though I loved Him with all my heart and still felt Him when I sang. In the dressing room after the concert or lying in my bunk on the bus, I kept pleading with Him for help, just as I did when I was twelve years old in the dark at my dad's church.

When Tori was on the road with us, I would never drink. But when she wasn't, I would keep a fifth hidden in my bunk. I justified it by telling myself that it helped me get to sleep after driving all night. I kept telling myself that I'd never ever be like my dad. But I secretly wondered if this was how he got started.

I had turned into a liar and it was killing me. But not enough to stop.

I CRY

When peace cannot be found
and sleep won't visit me tonight
a restless mind that I can't tame
I walk the floor I call Your name
Finally silence and the tears begin to fall

I cry and You're the one who hears me calling
I fall so easily but You're there to catch me
say the words that heal me
I'm safe when I'm with You
You touch my eyes and I can see

Oh the comfort that You bring
when nothing else can reach inside
sympathetic friends are all around
their soothing words fall to the ground
in silence I feel You here with me

(lyrics by Russ & Tori Taff, and James Hollihan)

TORI

When Russ was with The Imperials, I was the one that would maybe have a glass of wine with dinner if we went out to a restaurant. He never did. We'd go on a Sunday drive and he'd stop and get a Coke and I'd get a beer with pizza. I never had any thoughts about him drinking. We hardly ever had any alcohol around the house, so there weren't any missing bottles or weird behavior that made me question if anything was going on. But gradually, he started occasionally having a drink in front of me. One drink. If we were at a restaurant and we both had a glass of wine with dinner, when we got home I'd go upstairs and read and he'd go "run an errand" somewhere. After a while, he'd come in and yell up the stairs, "Hey, I'm back," and I'd say, "Okay." Then he'd come up and go to bed after I was asleep.

I don't think I put these words to it at the time, but I started sensing that Russ was becoming secretive. That he was hiding something. I saw it come out as anger. It wasn't directed toward me, he kept it tightly reined in, but he was wound pretty tightly. I had never felt frightened about his depression, just concerned. But now I felt something dark and shadowy in him for the first time.

He was moody, deeply but quietly angry, balled up like a fist. Turned inward. I could feel our marriage crumbling, but I couldn't identify the enemy. I couldn't see it was alcohol because I never saw him drunk. He had already been diagnosed with depression, so I just thought we were in the middle of a serious depressive episode.

As the attention intensified and Russ' career trajectory was taking off, I thought, *here we go. This is the second part of the adventure.* We had The Imperials part, and then all of a sudden, now the focus was solely on Russ. We were going places we hadn't gone before, more money was coming in. The touring got bigger, the band got bigger, the headaches got bigger. What I now know that I didn't know then, was that his spiral into addiction—hand in hand with depression—was getting bigger, too.

There were these incredibly confusing mixed signals going on at all times—big highs, like a successful album and tour, immediately followed by a drop into sullenness and despair. Most of the time he was restless and antsy. He'd always be wanting to get up and go someplace else. But whatever he was looking for, he wasn't finding it. And that was a microcosm of what was happening in our relationship.

It was literally the best of times and the worst of times. His career was at its zenith and he was disappearing, slipping farther away from me each day. I could never understand where all of the misery was coming from because I didn't know his secret life. I didn't know how disgusted he was with himself. I didn't know how angry he was with God.

Michael W. Smith

So, you get the awards. I've had them over the years— Grammys, American Music Awards, however many Dove Awards. It wears off. It doesn't last. And eventually everybody will forget the show. It doesn't fill the void. You think it will. But it's a never-ending cycle that will suck the life out of you.

I started pulling away from him, too. It was discouraging to try to help him feel better and watch my best efforts fall flat. He used to love the Christmas season, he started listening to Christmas music in August and I bet we watched *White Christmas* and *Miracle on 34th Street* a thousand times. One year, I took the eight hundred dollars that I had saved up from some modeling jobs with local department stores and spent every penny of it on Christmas decorations for the house. When he came home and walked in the door, it looked like Macy's Holiday Parade had exploded all over our living room.

Russ smiled and made the appropriate appreciative comments, then disappeared up the stairs to his office. I don't
think he ever mentioned it again.

I stopped going out on the road with him as much. Russ
would purposely pick a fight with me, arguing unreasonably
until I was completely discombobulated. And then of course I
wouldn't want to go jump on a bus with him since he had just
been such a jerk for the past week. So, mission accomplished,
he could go out by himself and drink without worrying about
me getting suspicious.

Any good alcoholic worth their salt knows how to knock
you emotionally off balance. Because that's what addiction
does to survive. If someone's going to hold them accountable,
they need to be away from that person. Russ knew that if I
knew how bad it was, I would either leave him, or I'd treat
it like the emergency it was. I'd be running around yelling,
"Your hair's on fire!"

His emotional seesaw behavior totally confused me, and
I'd fall for it every time. Because when he was nice, the sunshine came out. Then when he withdrew that love, which is
what it felt like, I'd be like, "What did I do?"

Russ: *That's what I was taught growing up.*

I'd say, "Russ, we need to talk about what's going on with
us." And we would. Ad nauseam, infinity. But there wasn't
an answer to it. I'd walk away feeling somewhat mollified,
because at least we were talking, which is exactly what he was
trying to accomplish. He learned to get me off his back by

letting me ramble on about my fears and feelings, and then pretend like he was taking it all to heart.

Here's the deal, too. I'm not a stupid person. I'm not a blind person. I'm not an incredibly naive person. When I first heard people talk about the part that denial plays in alcoholic relationships, I didn't think that applied to me. I wasn't trying to ignore the symptoms, I was trying to figure them out. But the reality was that I so badly wanted it all to be okay that I wouldn't let my mind dwell on the darkest possibilities.

I ended up shadowboxing. I didn't know what I was swinging at. I didn't have a plausible explanation. It's not like he was staggering in the door and throwing up on our couch. There wasn't anything to point at and go, *that's it*. It was just this thing that seemed to be encroaching into our lives and stealing him away. And it didn't have a name.

To further muddy the waters, I found out that Russ had started smoking. That made absolutely no sense to me. "You're a singer! What are you doing to your throat? How ridiculously self-destructive can you be?" He said he started smoking to help him stay awake while he drove the bus through the night. "You know how addictive smoking is. Why would you play around with something that could end up seriously hurting you?" But that was a literal smokescreen to hide what was really going on. When I'd see the handful of breath mints in his pocket or find a bottle of mouthwash under the car seat, I'd grit my teeth and think, *he's trying to disguise the smell of those stupid cigarettes.* To this day, I have kind of a knee-jerk negative reaction to smoking because that was the first visible evidence in my marriage of lying, covering up, and promising to quit. To me at that time, the face of addiction was cigarettes.

I never seriously wondered if I was the cause of his depression, but I did think that maybe I needed to try harder to be a good wife. Every once in a while, I'd sit down across from him and take his hand and ask, "Russ, are you happy with our life? With me?" He'd always say, "Yeah, yeah, I'm happy and I love you." But one night I kept pushing him, saying, "It just seems like something's very wrong." And he finally got irritated and said, "Well, if you really want to know, sometimes I just get so sick of all the stress that...I'll go out and get a drink of something to calm me down."

I was astounded. He'd never talked about anything like that before, and I'd sure never seen any evidence of it. It felt as if he was trying to tell me something without really saying it. "What are you talking about? Drink what?" I asked.

He said, "Vodka."

This little cheerleader was getting heated up quickly. This could not possibly be happening. "What? Where? We don't have vodka here, and I know you don't on the road."

Russ dropped his head, "In the car. Sometimes I keep it in the car."

Of course, I marched right out to the car. "Show me!" I insisted.

He defiantly said, "You really want to see it?"

He opened the trunk. He dug around in there and pulled out a bottle. I'm standing there looking at him, looking at the bottle, and my mind is spinning so fast. The TILT sign in my brain is flashing...what in the wide world? He looked at me standing there with my mouth agape and said, "What?"

Just a reminder, I'm actually a pretty peaceful person. I may have a mouth on me, but I hate to fight. I'm not a screamer and I don't throw dishes. But I was trembling, I was so mad. "I honestly want to hit you right now. Why would you risk bringing something into our life that destroyed your entire family? Are you insane?" I just kept repeating, "You're going to ruin this."

I knew there was this deep well of pain inside of him. It was bottomless, and it was formidable. But I couldn't understand why he would willingly court destruction. "That's like having a snake in the trunk. You think you can carry a snake into the house or go out and visit it in your car and you're not going to get bit?"

My reaction got his attention. The message I *thought* I was giving him was, "This is how seriously I'm taking this and how important it is to me. Please, don't do this to us." It never occurred to me that this was something he couldn't control. I felt sure that if he realized how scared and hurt I was, he would stop immediately.

But the message the alcoholic Russ heard was, "I really need to hide this better." I was trying to make him understand how dangerous drinking could be for him. He was trying to hint at his darkest truth, to see if I could handle it. And I completely freaked out on him. He got his answer loud and clear—it was not safe to talk to me about this. So, he just went further underground.

GOD ONLY KNOWS

Where do you draw the line
Between wrong and right
How close to the edge will you go
How does your heart define
The day from night
Shades of the truth and shades of a lie
You're living in shadows where
No one can see through your soul

Two restless eyes, avoiding mine
Signal a warning
There's trouble in disguise

God only knows what lies below
What sin is buried there
God only knows what doesn't show
What you refuse to share

How can I be a friend
And fail to see
Guilt robbing you of your joy
We used to cleanse our hearts, reveal our pain
Healing would always come
To both of us, but now

God only knows what lies below
What sin is buried there
God only knows what doesn't show
What you refuse to share

I'm not casting stones
I just want to know what you're holding in

(lyrics Russ & Tori Taff)

TORI

Russ was trapped in classic self-medicating. It's "I don't want to feel this. I need something outside of me to make these feelings go away." We were woefully uninformed about what we were up against. We did not have a clue there was such a strong genetic link with children of alcoholics, especially male to male. We were operating out of all the knowledge we had, our love for each other, and our belief in a power greater than ourselves that we were entrusting our lives to. And I felt sure that God would never let something horrible like alcoholism happen to us because we really loved Him and wanted to serve Him.

Years later we had a doctor explain that there's a disorder called dysthymia, which is basically a long-term, chronic form of depression that causes people to lose interest in normal daily activities, have low self-esteem, and feelings of inadequacy and hopelessness. He said Russ probably suffered from it most of his life. It's quite common with kids who grew up with trauma because trauma chemically changes your brain. The doctor said this low level of depression and addiction go hand in hand.

Over time, the depression and alcohol absolutely sucked the life out of that young couple who were so in love, living a life full of adventure and possibilities. Emotionally, the one person who had always been my safe place, my partner in crime, my beloved companion…that person became virtually unrecognizable to me. It was rapidly getting to the point where I wondered if we were going to survive this.

RUSS

I had no tools. I didn't know why this was happening. I spent hours and hours crying and begging God to help me. I had no way to deal with any of this, except for how I was taught to fast and pray. I went through a period of time thinking, "Am I demon possessed? I'm asking God for help and I'm not getting anything. He's not taking away this desire." That's what I thought healing would look like—the desire to drink would just magically go away, along with the anxiety and negative voices. But the way I was raised to earn God's attention was not working. I started thinking I must really be out of His will if He's still not responding after all of this praying, fasting, and Bible reading I'm doing. Now mind you, this is coming from someone who was secretly consuming a lot of mind-altering alcohol. But I didn't really understand the pathology of depression. I wish I would've known better sooner, but I'm thankful that I do now. Antidepressants don't always completely fix the problem, but they can help treat it.

When you're in a depressive state, you're all alone in your head. It's hard to see what is true and what is not true. There have been times that I know it has really scared Tori because it's like I'm paralyzed, hollow inside with no feelings. Sometimes I would just sit and stare at the wall. And then after a few months it would start to lift again.

The crazy thing is that I knew alcohol makes depression worse. But I would always opt for a few hours of relief versus living in hell for eleven months of the year.

To Tori, I was not the person who had always loved and delighted in her. I was a stranger. I was dealing with a whole lot of pain without any knowledge of how to help myself. But I was willing to do anything to learn.

TORI

I can't emphasize enough how well Russ hid his actual drinking for so many years. Granted, that was something that he literally learned at his father's knee, but he was dang good at it. I was helplessly watching him withdraw and withdraw, isolate and isolate. It was like seeing someone you love fade from color to black and white, then start fading out of the picture all together.

I tried everything I thought could possibly help, though I didn't have any real tools, either. I cried, I explained, I reasoned. I tried to sit down and talk it out. Anything to try to engage him, appeal to him. The more I came in after him, the more he would retreat.

I learned there are two kinds of numb for Russ. One is the numb of driving the bus all night and being so worn out you're not able to feel God when you sang. That's a bad numb. But then there's the numb that came with alcohol, when the voices, memories, and self-hatred would rise up, and you can drink them into silence.

These are concepts that were so hard for me to understand because I want to feel everything all the time. For Russ, there was an exhausted, flat-line numb, and then there was a blessed relief numb—two different things.

* * * * *

Jim Murray, The Imperials

I have to be honest, when it comes to Russ' alcoholism, I was not aware of it at all. I never saw Russ when he seemed off or out of control in any way. It never dawned on me to ask, "Are you drinking?" We had talked about his upbringing, and I remember he told me that at one point when he was a teenager he and his brother thought about just going out and doing everything their father always told them not to do—every sin known to man. He said, "Dad did it, but then he told us how bad it was. We thought maybe we ought to go see what the big deal was!" But I don't think he ever did. He must have done a good job of hiding his drinking which was fine because I surely didn't want to know. I wouldn't have been able to handle that. But it does explain why I was sometimes puzzled by his actions and things he would say. It kind of gave me an answer, in that sense.

It's only been recently that I've been able to really understand where he was coming from and how he dealt with it. I wish I had known. There were so many things that if I had a chance to do it over, I would say something or maybe be more compassionate than I was.

I really do love Russ. I know he's been through a lot, but he's just a special person. When he loves you, he loves you all the way. And Tori is just a sweetheart. She's so much fun. There is no telling what Tori's going to say. I guess the reason I enjoy her so much is because my late wife was the same way. With Loretta, you didn't have to ask her, "What do you think?" She's already told you what she thought. And when she walked in the room, just like Tori does, my wife lit up the room.

TORI

Lying is the cruelest thing you can do to your spouse. I totally understand that it's impossible to be an addict and *not* lie—it's how the addiction stays alive. When Russ repeatedly lied to me, it sent me tumbling through the entire gamut of emotions that every person who's ever been lied to experiences. Rage. Betrayal. Grief. Confusion. "How stupid do you think I am? I trusted you!" One of the worst parts was that it made me doubt myself. I would suppress all my gut feelings that were screaming at me saying something was very, very wrong because the man I loved was looking me in the eye and telling me what I felt wasn't based in reality. So, I'd tell myself, "Maybe I'm just being overly dramatic. Not everyone is happy all the time, this will pass."

It took me about as long to forgive myself and trust my judgment again as it did for me to forgive him and trust him. Something died in me towards him during that time, I'm not going to lie.

One of the most loving things God ever did for me was to give me Matt Timm for a brother. He is a child psychologist and activist in Nashville and one of the wisest, most soulful men I have ever known. I'm the youngest of six and he's the next to the oldest, so there's a good age span between us. We didn't really grow up together because he was already in college while I was still little, so we actually formed a bond and a friendship when we were adults. Matt had been married to an alcoholic and subsequently divorced. Along the way he got into Al-Anon, which is a support group for people whose lives have been affected by someone else's drinking.

Matt became a lifeline for me. He was a calm, stabilizing force when my whole world was blowing up. He gave thoughtful, measured responses to my frantic, endless questions. He never spouted advice or offered easy answers, he challenged me to dig deep and be unflinchingly honest with myself. And amazingly, he was somehow able to simultaneously be the one person both Russ and I felt completely safe with—we both knew we could tell Matt anything and he would never betray our confidences. I still don't know how he did that.

Before Russ was officially diagnosed, I told Matt I thought Russ was displaying some alcoholic-type attitudes and behaviors because he was raised by one. Matt said, "I'll say this one time. I think Al-Anon would be good for you." I'm not a joiner. I don't want to sell Amway, I don't want to be in the PTO, and Al-Anon is certainly not a club I wanted to be a part of. But I trusted Matt with all of my heart. So, I started going to Al-Anon before I even knew Russ was an alcoholic.

There was one bizarre Christmas trip home that finally brought things to a head. We went to Arkansas like we always do for the holidays. We stayed at my parent's house and would go back and forth to Mama June's house, too. Russ was just all over the place emotionally, even more than his usual unsettled self. I was always baffled and secretly more than a little hurt that Russ never completely settled in and embraced being a part of my incredibly loving and colorful family. If I married into my family, I'd feel like I hit the lottery! Even with the Smedleys, his "family of choice" as we called them, it always felt like he was sort of hovering on the fringes, restless and skittish. Both sides loved and accepted Russ completely. But it's like he had an invisible shield up in front of him that kept their love from penetrating his defenses.

This particular Christmas, he was completely erratic, leaving my parent's house to go spend time in Hot Springs with Bud and June, then exiting there shortly after he arrived and driving the forty-five minutes back to Benton to be miserable there. He stayed through Christmas morning, then inexplicably decided to leave early and head back to Nashville by himself. I was thoroughly confused and irritated, so I decided to call my brother Matt. Even though I knew he would never betray any of the private things Russ had confided in him, I also knew he would tell me the truth.

"Okay, Matt, we've talked about alcoholic tendencies, behaviors, patterns. Am I actually dealing with active alcoholism, here?"

There was a pause and he said, "Yeah, honey, you are."

I exhaled, "Right." I put the phone down and said out loud, "I'm married to an alcoholic. Russ is an alcoholic."

RUSS

God began to bring people into my life that started to recognize what was going on with me. The first one was Mama June. We were at the Arlington Hotel in Hot Springs and she and I met for coffee. She risked our relationship because she didn't know how I would respond. She said, "Russ, I think you have a drinking problem."

If it had been anybody else but her, I would have just blown it off with, "Hey, you don't even know what a drinking problem is. If you had grown up in the house I did, you'd know what alcoholism looked like."

Mama June hadn't seen me drink, but she saw me changing. My smile was gone. There was no joy, no feel-good place. She and Bud had a friend with a bad alcohol problem and he had gotten sober. They began to see in me the same signs this other guy was showing before he got help—the isolation, the personality shift, the hiding. I was emotionally unstable and unpredictable.

She said to me, "I know what you're doing. And it's having a very destructive effect on you. You're developing some really negative patterns."

I denied it, of course. "No, I'm just having a few beers now and then." But she wouldn't let me go. She said, "No, your personality has changed. I don't know who you are anymore."

It broke my heart. I got so angry and defensive. "How dare you?" I responded.

Mama June just looked at me with the most compassionate, understanding eyes. I knew she loved me. She saw what was going on and my charade was up. I felt wretched for trying to pull one over on this incredible person I cared for so deeply. It brings me to tears today just thinking about her great love and my insolence.

I didn't quit drinking that day, but my eyes were starting to open. It was harder and harder to deny the fact that I was destroying everything around me. I was destroying my relationship with Tori, I was destroying my relationship with June and Bud, and I was destroying my career. I was surrounded by wreckage and I had caused it.

A short while after, I was in Memphis for a show. I was on my face on the dressing room floor, laying prostrate, begging God, "Kill me or heal me. I can't live this way anymore." I cried and cried uncontrollably. And somewhere in the back of my mind I heard a voice, His voice, and He said, "I love you." That made me cry even more because with the religion I was raised in, I fully expected wrath and judgment. All I got back was "I love you."

TORI

Russ was starting to come to terms with the idea that he had a problem. He finally said, "I've been drinking some and I know I can't do that with my family history and my genetics. I know it's a problem…I think I want to go to an AA meeting."

Matt connected Russ with a guy who took him to his first meeting in Nashville, one that a lot of artists and musicians attended. And I continued going to Al-Anon meetings. I even went through a family program at Cumberland Heights, a treatment center here in Nashville, before Russ ever went to treatment. Knowledge is power and I knew I needed all the information I could get. I called and said, "Could I pay the money and go through the family week even if I don't have somebody in treatment?" They said yes, and I did.

That spring, we were planning to go on the road together for another leg of his big *Medals* tour. Russ was starting to act really bizarre. We had some kind of blow up, he was being so sarcastic and unreasonable. My gut was saying that something wasn't right. I finally said, "Are you drinking again?" and he said, "I had a couple of drinks, just one time—I had a bad night and I was trying to sleep."

That's when I said, "I'm not going on this tour with you."

He said, "I'm not going to drink on the road. I'm back going to meetings, and I'll go to meetings on the road."

I had enough Al-Anon to know that I couldn't control whether he was going to drink or not. I knew I had to do whatever I could to stay sane myself, even if it meant letting Russ head out on tour in the kind of shape he was in.

I told him, "You're going to do what you're going to do whether I'm with you or not. I'm not going to make myself crazy trying to follow you around and figure out if you're sneaking drinks. So, go act like a rock star. Knock yourself out."

I also decided I needed to cut off all contact with him. "I can't deal with you calling me and acting like everything's fine when I have no way of knowing what's really happening. And I can't call you every day and ask, 'What are you doing?'" I said, "You won't tell me the truth if you're drinking, anyway. And if you say you're not drinking, I won't believe you even if it's the truth. This is absolutely a no-win situation for me. So, I'm not going to play."

He left for the tour without me. He was completely out of control at this point. In true alcoholic fashion, he engineered the blow-up between us to push me away so that he would be free to do whatever he wanted. We now look back and refer to that tour, not fondly, as the "drunk tour." It was the first time I actually knew for a fact that he was drinking on the road. He later told me it wasn't every night and it was never before he went on stage. But he was spiraling.

Bonnie Keen

I've traveled and recorded with Russ singing backup vocals for years. But more than working together, our personal lives were intertwined. Russ and Tori are family—we've been through so much together that you wouldn't believe it if I told you. Early on, it felt like Russ was struggling to hold onto God. But as we spent more time together as friends, I realized it wasn't that, but instead, he was fighting hard to reconcile his past with his present. At times on the road I saw glimpses of his pain. I truly believe it's this struggle that allows his powerhouse talent to resonate with the best and worst of the human experience, as if he's singing with a voice of a thousand souls.

Even though we were close, I didn't realize the level of his suffering.

I didn't know his life was literally slipping away, eroding in a prison of a hidden disease.

I met him in Little Rock at the end of the tour. All our families and friends were there, but they didn't know what had been going on. I told him that night, "Russ, I can't let you come back to the house unless we get into some kind of intensive therapy." He grudgingly agreed, but decided he wanted to go spend some time at Bud and June's house in Hot Springs first. He said he would go to meetings there and think hard about what he really wanted and what he was willing to do to get it. My goal was to get him into some kind of treatment.

Now remember, all of this was taking place while Russ was at the top of his career as an artist. He had just won a Grammy for his debut album with the huge song "We Will Stand." He was touring the *Medals* album with an amazing band and full production. He was selling out venues, radio airplay, and record sales were blowing up. Lots of opportunities were flying at us, everybody wanted a piece of him. It was bigger than we could have ever dreamed. But somehow it wasn't fixing the broken places. It makes me sad to think that Russ was never really able to enjoy much of it. But knowing what I know now, it makes sense.

When he got back to Nashville, we met with our therapist and basically had a showdown in her office. Russ didn't come home that night. But the next day, our friend Dan drove him to his first stint in a treatment center just outside of Knoxville. It was a center that specializes in treating impaired physicians, but our therapist felt like this would be the right fit for Russ. Doctors are looked up to and treated better than most people and they are in a position of authority that is hard to challenge. There were certainly some parallels there.

The timing could not have been worse. Russ and the band were scheduled to leave in ten days for an extended series of concerts across Australia. We had no other choice than to cancel the entire tour and claim "family crisis"—which was true enough, but also vague enough that it sounded like it could be his family in California or something. Our beloved no-nonsense manager Zach stepped in and told me not to worry about anything other than taking care of myself. He would deal with everything else. It was devastating for us, but even more so for all the people who would be financially affected by Russ pulling out at the last minute. I felt so guilty and I was also scared to death someone would find out the real reason.

After the thirty-day stint in rehab, Russ left Knoxville and flew straight to Buffalo to kick off a twenty-three-city tour he was headlining with Sheila Walsh and Mylon LeFevre & Broken Heart. I met him there with the band. Only a handful of people closest to us really knew what had happened and where he'd been. There were rumors of some sort of "break-down," but as Zach told me in his pragmatic way, "Don't waste energy over things you can't control. If people find out, they find out. We'll deal with it then." Russ walked off the plane wearing a pair of black moccasins he had made in arts and crafts therapy at the treatment center. Later, we laughingly referred to them as his "twenty-five-thousand-dollar house shoes" because that's how much of our savings we emptied out to pay for his treatment. Wasn't that funny at the time.

After the tour, Russ settled into his sobriety, attending meetings, going to therapy, and diligently working on getting better. After a few years, the memories of just how bad it had been and how close we had come to losing it all gradually faded for both of us. I cautiously began to make plans for our future, even daring to allow myself to think about starting a family. We always knew we wanted children—well, at least I did. Russ told me years later that he was secretly terrified to be a father because he was convinced he wouldn't be any good at it. We had always said we would wait to have a baby until Russ' career had reached the point where we could afford to cut down on touring and have a home life. It was going to be an adjustment for both of us, but mostly me. I loved life on the road. I had dreamed of traveling on a bus with a band since I was in the sixth grade and fell in love with Davy Jones and The Monkees. But I was in my mid-thirties now and the clock was ticking. Loudly.

At the risk of sounding indelicate, I figured after waiting for fifteen years, we ought to be able to knock this pregnancy thing out in about fifteen minutes. Unfortunately, it didn't work that way. After months of trying, we finally ended up in a fertility clinic undergoing a series of invasive (for me) and embarrassing (for Russ) tests. They couldn't find anything wrong with either of us, which was even more frustrating. Russ' theory was that my eggs were so old they had to use walkers and his swimmers were stopping for a smoke break along the way, so they just kept missing each other. That weird sense of humor, by the way, is a large part of why we are still together.

After a lot of fervent prayer and more than a little help from modern medicine, Madeleine Rose Taff came into our world on June 27, 1992. Since my labor lasted approximately a year and a half (slight exaggeration), our Arkansas loved ones were able to make the drive to Nashville just in time for the big event. I gave birth surrounded by my favorite women in the world: my mom, my two sisters, and Mama June. It was surreal, holy, and perfect. When Maddie Rose was only a few minutes old, she delighted the doctors by slowly and deliberately turning her head towards Russ when he started softly singing, "Buffalo gal, won't you come out tonight?" I guess she wanted to see who'd been singing to my tummy for the last nine months.

Parenthood is absolutely the best thing that ever happened to us. Our family is a baby-crazy bunch, so bringing our new addition home to Arkansas for the first time was like bringing Christmas. Maddie Rose, in addition to being gorgeous and perfect, was also, as my mom used to say, "an amiable child." She was a good little traveler and we took her on lots of family trips, even on the bus sometimes. She was properly doted on by a large and loving assortment of aunts, uncles, cousins, in-laws, out-laws, and grandparents. It was the happiest of times.

Russ, despite his secret misgivings, was an excellent father—very hands-on, involved, and fearless. He was gentle and loving with Maddie, and they developed a strong connection very early on. From the time she was still a baby in arms, she would tear up whenever she heard Russ sing. When she was three and he was downstairs rehearsing "The Lord's Prayer" for a friend's wedding, I found her in her room sitting on the side of her bed and crying. When I asked her what was wrong, she said, "Nothing. I'm just feeling my feelings." I remember her favorite pre-school teacher, Ms. Mary, telling me once, "Maddie Rose looks more like you on the outside, but she is more like Russ on the inside." She was right.

Maddie Rose Taff, Daughter

Some of my earliest memories are being in the recording studio with Dad. I also went to see him in concerts a lot when I was little which was a weird but fun way to grow up. He's your sweet, funny Daddy and you love him, but then you see him up on stage singing with this crazy loud voice, and thousands of other people are loving him, too. You kind of feel like you're sharing him, but I remember even as a child just being so proud.

One of my favorite things to do with Dad is going for walks at Radnor Lake and talking about God. Even when it's just him and I, he will get choked up talking about the love of God. When I see him on stage, it's the same dad that I grew up with. He's speaking from the heart.

We were having so much fun with Maddie Rose, we wanted to do it again. Russ and I went straight back to the fertility specialists and to our delight, got pregnant after only one procedure. When I was almost three months along, we were heading down to Arkansas for my twentieth high school reunion—I figured I'd probably be the only former cheerleader there in maternity clothes—and stopped by the doctor's office on our way out of town for my monthly check-up. We were so excited about being able to hear the heartbeat for the first time, but as Russ and I held hands and listened, the only thing we heard was the whirring of the ultrasound machine as the increasingly concerned technician moved it repeatedly back and forth across my stomach. I still remember the sympathetic, somber face of the doctor saying words like "blighted ovum" and "no discernible cause." We drove the seven hours home in shock, tears coursing down both our faces.

RUSS

It took us a solid year of more testing and more procedures before we finally got pregnant again. Tori's ever-hopeful personality was severely tested. It was so hard to see her bitter disappointment, month after month. At one point I gently told her I thought we should maybe stop trying and start looking into adoption, but wouldn't you know it, that's the very month we got the good news. Tori was over the moon. She turned forty that June, nine months pregnant with our Charlotte. And on July 17, 1996, a tiny (5 lbs. 15 oz.) but very loud baby girl arrived, and our little family was complete.

TORI

I'm eternally grateful we didn't give up. I wouldn't have missed Charlo for the world. She is absolutely, as Maddie Rose once described her, "delightfully strange and wise beyond her years." Charlotte inherited my dad's temperament—we used to call him Don "Just Happy to Be Here" Timm. She holds the family record for best Halloween costumes. Her favorite was the shark with legs dangling out of its mouth, but I personally preferred the year she was sixteen months old and we dressed her up like the NFL Rainbow Man with a multi-colored clown wig on and "John 3:16" scrawled across her tiny bare chest. Even though Russ is 100 percent equally their parent too, I have always referred to Maddie and Charlotte as "my girls." It took a lot to get them here, but it was all worth it. And I kind of love the fact that Russ is living in a house full of estrogen—even our pets are female!

Charlotte Taff, Daughter

A lot of people meet me, shake my hand, and say, "Oh my gosh, you're Russ Taff's daughter! What's it like living with him?" Well, it's actually pretty quiet. He doesn't sing around the house, he naps on the couch, and I'm usually there beside him playing video games.

The first thing I love about Dad is his humor—his smartassness. We could be in the worst situation possible, but he's still able to crack a joke and make us laugh about it. Sometimes now I will say something off the wall or make a funny self-deprecating comment and when he laughs, I'll say, "I learned it from you."

I've always known I have a dad who loves me more than anything. Before Maddie and I were born, Dad went to Mama June. He was terrified about having kids because of what he went through. He said, "I just don't want to mess them up. How am I supposed to handle this?" She stopped him and said, "You just have to love them as much as you can." And that's exactly what he's been doing since I was a little girl.

The early years with the girls were some of our best. But the shadow of depression still lingered around Russ, and there

were times when his symptoms would overwhelm his medication. Then there would be a tense period, sometimes weeks
or even months at a time, while the doctors tried to come up
with a combination of meds that would give him some relief.
He began suffering from almost daily migraines, which made
traveling and singing even more challenging. I felt like Russ
was losing ground, and there was another distant warning bell
going off in my head.

Then in 1997, we got word that his father's health, which
had been declining, had taken a sharp turn. I knew that Russ
was craving some kind of closure with his dad or even just an
acknowledgement of the pain he had caused. We tried desperately to get him on a flight to California in time, but his father
passed away while the plane was still in the air. There was not
going to be any deathbed resolution.

LONG HARD ROAD

We loved each other so much
Oh, but no so very well
And now that we've run out of time
I guess time will never tell
So I'll picture you surrounded by all the love and grace
That I watched you run from all your living days
So I'll surrender you to a higher plan
Until we can talk it over man to man

And in the New Jerusalem
With all our defenses down
You will say the words I long to hear
And healing will be found
You will open up your arms with love

And finally hold me close
And we will end this long hard road

Don't think that this is over, don't think that this is solved
Just because you're not around any more
Doesn't mean you're not involved
As I sit alone asking why, I wonder if you cried too
Did you know all was forgiven
Did you know that I loved you

There always was this dance between us
Some day there'll be a second chance
I believe it

(lyrics by Russ & Tori Taff)

Though Russ had been sober for over ten years, the hurricane of emotions that resurfaced from the death of his father triggered a relapse. When I realized what was happening, it was like being kicked in the stomach. I met with our therapist Dr. David McMillan and we set up an intervention. My brother Matt, my best friend Bonnie, Zach, Russ' AA sponsor, and several of our closest friends got together in David's office and confronted Russ. They told him how much they loved him, and how much they didn't want him to continue down this destructive path. My compassionate brother Matt said to Russ, "How many Grammys is it going to take before you feel loved? How many Dove Awards, how many sellout concerts? At what point does all of that make you feel like you're worth something? Because it doesn't seem to be working, does it?"

Matt's voice broke when said, "Every single person in this room knows how valuable you are except you. You're the only one in this room who doesn't get it."

Bill Gaither

Tori called me one day and said, "Bill, I need your help."

I said, "Help on what?" I may have heard the word "intervention" before, but it was the first time I had been involved in one. When I showed up that night with about fourteen other people, it was very uncomfortable for me. I knew Russ enough to know that I loved him. So, I asked Tori, "What are we supposed to do?"

She said, "Just be there as his friend."

I'll never forget listening to everyone as they went around the room and thinking *wow, they're being kind of hard on ol' Russ.* Of course, I had no idea how bad his drinking was, I had never seen any evidence of it.

After the meeting was over he left. I went out looking for him and said, "You okay?"

"Yeah, I'm okay," he said.

"You want to get something to eat?"

"Yeah."

Our relationship deepened considerably that night. I found myself apologizing to him because I knew how hard this had been on him. He said, "Don't apologize. I'm the problem, and this was necessary."

"What are you going to do?" I asked.

"Well, I'm going to do what they tell me to do because I need help."

The next day Russ entered treatment again, this time at Cumberland Heights, just outside of Nashville. The drive there was bleak, in spite of the beautiful farmland we were rolling past and the sweet sound of our two little girls playing in their car seats behind us. I had agonized over whether I should bring them, but Russ had never been away for thirty days before, and I thought if they could see where he would be staying, it might be less confusing for them. But Russ was staring out the window with tears rolling down his face, the girls were starting to look scared, and I was seriously second-guessing my decision.

Suddenly Maddie Rose squealed, "Mama, stop!" I slammed on the brakes and whirled around. "Look!" Maddie pointed over the hood of the car. "There's a turtle in the road. You almost murdered it, can you please go see if it's okay?"

Five minutes later we were back on the road towards Cumberland Heights again, except instead of tears and scared looks, there was excited chatter about what to name the new turtle (we settled on "Lucky"), where he could live (in a box in the backyard), and whether we should try to find him a wife (no). As we parked in front of the registration building, Maddie Rose looked around at the beautiful fields and woods surrounding the grounds and said reverently, "Wow, Daddy. You get to stay here? I bet this place is just *full* of turtles." I glanced skyward as I walked Russ into the intake desk. "I saw what You did there," I prayed. "Thank you."

There's not a simple answer to how I got through those days. A good Christian answer is "with prayer and God." That is the truth. But just praying and asking God to fix it wasn't changing it. My faith is part of who I am. It's not a choice that I make on a daily basis. I don't wake up and see if I am going to believe in God that day. But "faith without works is dead," and I certainly had some work to do on myself, too.

My main prayer during that time was to ask God to reach deep inside Russ, to connect with that part of Himself that lived in Russ' heart. Spirit to spirit, deep calling to deep. I knew He was the only one that could pierce through all the pain, anger, and addiction.

I was so furious that Russ was squandering who he was. I'm not talking about his voice, but about who he was inside. Russ, the man I fell in love with, who I admired and respected, was getting decimated and degraded and he was the one doing it. Russ has one of the kindest hearts of anyone I know, and he was acting like a reckless, out of control teenager—nobody was going to tell *him* what to do. It was taking everything in me to try to stay sane and lean in hard to my family, especially Matt, and amazing friends like Bonnie. Bonnie and I had been best friends for years and years. We met during our modeling days, and Russ and I had walked with her through her divorce and subsequent depression together. We were bonded for life. Bonnie celebrated me, even the parts of myself I was trying to work on, like my tendency to overanalyze things and talk them to death. She could always cheer me up and cheer me on. She was also steadfastly loving and compassionate toward Russ. But, she was getting increasingly scared for both of us.

It was like we were standing in front of an approaching train, and I was too busy yelling at him to get out of the way to look out for my own safety. There was a growing realization in me that I could not and would not stay in a marriage that was emotionally dangerous for me. I was also physically exhausted, stressed out from living in a state of high alert, taking Russ' emotional temperature one hundred times a day, and constantly trying to gauge how he was doing. The question I needed to be asking was not, "How can I help him get sober?" It was, "Should I still be here?"

I thought if I had any love left towards him at all, that meant I had to stay in the marriage and keep trying. One day

I had the revelation that, "Tori, you can love him…and leave him." I didn't have to stay until the love was gone. I may need to walk away if being there wasn't helping either one of us. That's not what I wanted, but I might not have a choice.

I remember one argument when I was angrily pleading with him, "This isn't who you are. It can be who you become if you stay on this road. You can ride this pony and be just another Taff who goes out in a haze of alcohol and a blaze of fury. But it's going to be a deliberate choice. It's not going to be because you don't know what's going on or you don't know where the help is. It will be a conscious choice to walk away from everything you know is right and everyone who loves you. And if that's the choice you continue to make, I won't be here. I'm not going to chain myself to someone who doesn't want to be healthy—because I do." Russ' anger, self-hatred, and helplessness were so intense at that point that he reared back and punched a hole in the wall.

I told Dr. McMillan, "You know what, I may not be able to do this. I may seriously need to get a divorce." He leaned back in his chair and said, "You're way too mad to get divorced. I see a lot of people in this office who are at that place, and believe me, this is not what it looks like. You may think you've got one foot out the door, but you're still way too engaged. You haven't given up on him yet."

I was almost disappointed by his answer. But he was right, I just couldn't believe that Russ would let himself self-destruct.

In 12-Step programs they say that an alcoholic does what an alcoholic does, and we add the words "to me." Russ' addiction felt like he was doing it to me. What I learned to do in Al-Anon, through listening to people's gut-wrenchingly painful stories, was to separate myself from what the other person was doing. It's not all about the alcoholic, it's not about trying to fix him or stop him. It's about recognizing that the only person on the face of the earth whose behavior, reactions, and emotions that I can control are my own.

I started to truly understand alcoholism as a disease. I used to think they just said that to make weak-willed people feel better about their lack of self-control. But I educated myself on the subject and learned that in 1956 the American Medical Association officially declared that addiction fit all the medical criteria for a primary, chronic, progressive, and sometimes fatal, brain disease. I wasn't trying to become an expert or anything, I just wanted to know what I was up against. I read about the pathology of an alcoholic's brain, the neurobiology of how alcohol affected them, and the psychological causes that can drive addiction. But Russ lying to me again and again and again made me feel crazy. My gut was telling me one thing, but this person I loved and trusted was looking me in the face and telling me that what my gut was feeling was not the truth.

RUSS

Even before I went to treatment the first time, God had brought several men into my life who had walked the road I was walking. These men told me about the value of going to Alcoholics Anonymous meetings. I had heard of AA at that time, but honestly, I thought it was basically a program for hopeless drunks living under an overpass. I didn't know yet that the disease of addiction is no respecter of persons and affects people from every economic, ethnic, and religious group in the world. When I first started sitting in those rooms and hearing their stories, I was blown away. The surface details may have been different, but their stories were just like mine. They kept saying how God and this program had helped them stop drinking. By going to those meetings and listening to people share, I started feeling a little bit of hope that maybe I could stop, too.

A lie that most of us live with is the one that says we are all so unique. As if there's nobody in the world with problems like I have. This lie keeps us in isolation, convinced no one will ever be able to understand us. But by being in those rooms, I learned I was wrong. I wasn't alone. Maybe some of my circumstances were different, but we all had so much in common.

Our counselor seemed to understand my situation and had some ideas on how to clean up the wreckage in my life. All of this was so foreign to me. I was raised up in a denomination where you prayed it away. You fasted it away. I began to meet and talk with this man and get really honest. Gut-wrenchingly honest. It took a lot for me to break out of that "don't talk outside the family" mindset, not to mention the people-pleaser in me that wanted everyone to always think I was wonderful. But as I began to talk with him, he would say, "That happened to you at six, and here it is at twelve, fifteen, and again now at thirty. Look at these patterns that have been established." I was starting to connect the dots on behaviors I had been baffled by my entire life.

I had to learn how to live again. Because I had lived the other way so long and it just wasn't working.

Amy Grant

Russ was struggling with alcohol on the "Unguarded" tour that we were on together, but I didn't know that. I remember a very few people within the music community privately saying, "I think he's crashing." Which is not necessarily a bad thing. We all crash in different ways. The journey of life is to experience life—doing it right, doing it wrong.

Some things were going on in Russ' life that I was just oblivious to until he told me years later. But when somebody's so talented and gifted, it's easy just to focus on their talent. And especially if their talent is generating income for other people, you just want to keep that going, whatever it takes.

I remember taking a long walk with Russ on our farm a few years ago. He was finding new language to talk about the consistent struggle of trying to make peace with the role his father had in his life. I've struggled with some of the same stuff Russ has struggled with, but because of the circumstances of my life, the pendulum didn't swing as wide. But I think every artistic or creative person battles a certain amount of inner chaos and uncertainty.

When it comes to struggle and marriage, nobody rides off into the sunset. There were ways that Russ' life was strong and beautiful where mine was derailing. It's not like I was his friend that had it all together. I was careening wildly off course and crashed and burned in my marriage to Gary. I lost my ability to value that relationship. Everybody's strong and weak in different places.

There's not a person that feels their spouse drifting away that doesn't say, "Am I going crazy? Is it just me?" I've had that conversation a dozen times with different women, family included, saying, "I think I'm going crazy because everything's not adding up here."

God has equal opportunity to be present whether a marriage works or doesn't. When you're under the crushing weight of multiple layers of failure, it's hard to resist the settling of God's presence on you saying, "You're loved,

loved, loved. Keep going." Even in the middle of this hell-hole I'm in...really? "Yep."

You have nothing left, and the snot-cry has come and gone, and it's only devastation. There is no good staying, and there's no good leaving, it's awful. Dying sounds even better than living. But God comes into that stillness. That experience changes everything. It changes how you see other people. It changes how you see success and failure. It changes how you experience God. It's a big dose of mercy.

Another one of our dearest friends over the past twenty-five years has been Reverend Becca Stevens. She's been an instrumental voice of truth and grace in our lives, and also one of our favorite people in the world. She's an Episcopal priest at St. Augustine's Chapel on the Vanderbilt campus here in Nashville, but also founder of Magdalene and Thistle Farms, which are amazing outreaches to help women who are survivors of trafficking, addiction, and prostitution. She and her husband Marcus moved in across the street from us and the four of us became good, good friends. Our lives started to weave together in so many ways. Marcus is an unbelievably talented singer and songwriter. Becca and Tori were both raising kids about the same ages. We were in and out of each other's houses all the time and even took vacations together. We became very involved in the Magdalene program and Thistle Farms, and Tori served on the board for ten years. But Becca's friendship became especially important as she helped me process parts of my journey, usually taking place during brisk walks around Radnor Lake or the different greenways around the city.

Rev. Becca Stevens—Magdalene, Thistle Farms, 2016 CNN Hero

We're so thankful for how Russ and Tori have always been there for the community of Thistle Farms. Whenever we wanted a fundraiser, Tori could organize it and Russ would sing. One night, I called Russ to help me go rescue a woman who had been trapped in prostitution. She desperately wanted to get out and needed a safe place for the night. I was checking her into a motel but didn't have a credit card. Russ showed up with his credit card so we could get her a room until we could find a treatment place for her. Picture Russ and I at the check-in desk with a woman from the streets. He said, "You know, if somebody sees me right now it probably wouldn't go over too well." I said, "Don't worry about it, Russ. It's only interesting to other people when it's really something scandalous. It's not news if you're just trying to love people and do the work of God."

Becca comes at Jesus in a completely different way than I had been raised. She truly believes that love heals, which is the motto of her women's programs. During our deep spiritual talks, we'd cover all kinds of topics. Some days we'd talk about God's unconditional love, or the frustrations of organized church, or grace. She became a close friend of both Tori and I, someone who would be there whenever we needed help.

During one of my relapses, Tori called Becca and asked if she could go pick me up. She found me sitting on a curb next to my car. Becca said, "Russ, you've got to come with us, we've got to get you some help." Even though I was intoxicated I still knew that I could trust her. That I was safe with her.

Loving and showing grace were the dominant forces in her life, not criticizing or shaming.

Like Becca has said, sometimes it's the right person being there at the right time, or the right phone call, the right word, that can really make a long-term difference in the outcome.

Rev. Becca Stevens

"Love heals" is distilling down into two words the truth about our lives and journey with Jesus. It's the quintessential message of the gospel. And I've seen this played out in Russ and Tori's life. They kept loving each other. They kept loving their Lord. They kept loving their children, believing that it would be healing for them. And they did it and they didn't give up. There were a lot of times they could have given up, either one of them, and they didn't. And I respect that so much. Because if you believe that love heals, that means you are willing to do the hard work. You're willing to do it day after day after day until it becomes years until you have a foundation upon which to build. Love heals isn't a miracle cure. It's a commitment to live and to love and to trust that we can make that journey towards wholeness. And that's what they've done.

They have a lot to teach people about how addictions can affect your life, and how much you can grow and learn from it. I love that they've made it through together with deep love and honesty, and that Russ really sees this journey as a spiritual struggle. He has wrestled with the demons and has been tended to by the angels out in the wilderness. And throughout all of his searching, he stayed hungry for spiritual life and sobriety. He still wants to figure out what is the best way to be part of God's plan for His people—to be a vessel for them to hear God's words.

SIX

GOING SOLO

I feel like we might need to take a little breather from all the heaviness of addiction, sobriety, relapses, treatment centers...*I know I could use one!* I'd love to tell you more about the music side of my life because it has been my heart and soul, only second to my family. So, let me back up a little bit to 1981 when I knew a professional change was a-coming.

As the word got around that I was leaving The Imperials, I began to hear a lot of people's opinions about my decision. Of course, no one had any idea about the inner-workings of the group, or my circumstances. A head honcho at our label, Word Records, came from Waco, Texas to quietly visit me. He didn't want anyone to know we were meeting. He said, "You know Russ, no one has left The Imperials and been successful." It felt like he was literally trying to scare me into staying in the group. Obviously, he had a stake in the matter—we were selling a lot of records for them at the time and *Priority* was just about to release. He didn't dissuade me, but I'd be lying if I said he didn't instill a little bit of fear in me. Not only was I was walking away from the biggest group out there, as well as a steady paycheck, but the possibility existed that I could fall on my face and never be heard from again.

This new adventure felt similar to when I left Hot Springs to go work for Jerry Savelle—I had no idea what was going to happen. Right as I was leaving the group, Tori and I wrote a song that came out of this place of venturing into the unknown.

This song started as a prayer to help quiet my heart:

BE STILL MY SOUL

Surrounded by the cares of life
Situations rise, they press against my soul
Desperate thoughts have blocked me in
Feels like I may lose control.
A Voice from somewhere inside of me
Brings comfort and fills my heart with courage
And lets me know that everything will be alright

Be still, my soul, and know that He is God
Stand quietly – He is the Lord
If God is for me who can be against me?
Be still, my soul, He is the Lord
Be still my soul and know that He is God

(words & music: Russ & Tori Taff)

I still go back to that song when a change is coming. You have to step out in faith even if you can't see solid ground. Like Abraham did when God called him out. He didn't have a clue where he was going. But God told him to move, so he packed up everything and just started moving with no clear destination. I have been asked to do that three times now.

A buzz was starting to build about me leaving. One of my last concerts with The Imperials was a performance at one of fancy balls held for President Ronald Reagan's inauguration. Tori and I knew we needed to clear our heads and pray for direction, so as soon as we got back from Washington, D.C. we took a little weekend getaway. "Okay, Lord, where do we go from here?"

When we got back in town, there were ninety-seven messages on my answering machine from promoters, record companies, and managers, with all kinds of offers and proposals. Talk about overwhelming.

I know this sounds kind of corny, but my honest desire was simply to sing for Jesus and let His spirit move in my concerts so that the audience felt it, were ministered, and encouraged. That's the highest calling there is—nothing better. I understood ministry and music, but these new opportunities would require a level of business acumen that I didn't have.

I got to know Zach Glickman the summer prior at a gathering of Christian artists in Estes Park, Colorado. He was not a member of the Christian faith, but a Jewish man from Baltimore who was a fish out of water in the middle of this CCM industry event. He was there to scope out the scene because he was managing Dion DiMucci (of Dion and the Belmonts), who had recently accepted Jesus and wanted to make a Christian record.

There was a panel discussion session that Tori and I wanted to hear, so we snuck in the back of the room and sat down. Behind a long table at the front sat a row of record label heads and industry execs, and the space in between was crammed with eager, aspiring Christian singers. Most of the questions had to do with how to land a record deal.

The panel experts shared some practical advice, but there was also a lot of, "We evaluate each artist's ministry, then we pray and ask God if we should sign them or not." From a far corner of the room a Baltimore accent spoke up and said, "Excuse me, but isn't the real bottom line whether or not you think an artist has the potential to sell a lot of records? I mean, your jobs depend on whether or not you make money for the record companies. It doesn't seem fair to tell these young people that God tells you who to sign because what if they don't sell and you have to drop them? Did God change His mind?" There was a hush that came over the room. I already knew that sometimes when Christians talk business, things like motives and profit margins can get a little over-spiritualized. But this was the first time I had ever heard anybody politely call that out. I turned to Tori and whispered, "I want to meet that guy."

I signed my first solo record with Word Records in 1981. It was a very good deal, thanks to Zach. I was so grateful for his willingness to guide me because I had no idea how to approach a record label—they would've eaten me alive. If I had just walked in as a novice saying, "I want to sing for Jesus," I could have ended up signing something ridiculous. Zach said, "When you sign a record deal, this is what's expected and these are some of the dangers." He laid it all out so clear for me. There was no sneaking around meeting behind other people's backs or that whole posturing thing that felt so unnecessary to me. Zach helped me do my homework, then he told me, "Pray about it, decide where you want to be, and I'll go make the deal."

After six months, Zach said, "I'm going to invest in you. I'll give you advice and help you with contracts for free, but there will come a time when it's so big, you won't be able to handle it by yourself and then we'll talk about paying me." He knew money was tight and expenses were high. People come to a concert and they see you perform but they don't realize how many people it takes to get you there. I needed a band, a road manager, and transportation. James had left The Imperials with me and became my band leader, helping me put together an incredible group of musicians, but they had to get paid. So, for the first four years of my career Zach did all the work for nothing. But after *Walls of Glass* came out and we started selling product and the crowds started getting bigger, I brought him on as my business manager and was able to pay him a percentage. We called Zach our Jewish Mother— he was loud, pushy, loyal, and loving. He always told me the truth and he didn't sugar-coat it. Tori and I considered him family. Our business relationship lasted over thirty years until his death in 2015.

It was rough going there at the start. I had all these expenses right off the bat with no product to sell on the record table— that'd be another two years. And The Imperials wouldn't let me sell any of the records we had done together. How I made it work was that I would go out and do concerts, come back home, pay the band, and then go to the bank to get a ninety-day loan. Those first two years were spent borrowing and paying back. It was a juggling act, hoping we could stay afloat.

Michael Omartian was going to produce my first record. He had done the last two Imperial's records—*One More Song For You* and *Priority*. He and I had really clicked. For the previous Imperials records, the producers would find the songs and create the tracks, then we'd step off the bus and record the vocals in five days. Then we'd be back on the bus. I always felt the frustration of that because I wanted to learn more about creating different sounds, even specific snare or guitar sounds.

Working with Michael on those records was great because a couple of times Tori and I even stayed over at their house while the other guys went home to their families. It was such a thrill because I had never been around a project from the beginning to end like that. To start with an idea for a song that you begin to water until it starts to grow. And it gets bigger and bigger. And then you bring in excellent musicians and this idea turns into an incredible song. It was so exciting. I was like a kid in a candy store. I had waited my whole life for this.

Around this time, Michael had produced a new artist named Christopher Cross, who had huge success with "Sailing," winning multiple Grammys and selling millions of records. We were just about to start my record and Michael gets a call from Warner Brothers saying, "I don't care what you're doing. We need another Christopher Cross record."

I couldn't wait for another eighteen months for him to finish that project, so Michael introduced me to Bill Schnee, who was a legend in his own right. I didn't want my solo record to sound like The Imperials. I didn't want a snare sound that sounded like The Imperials. The sounds Bill created, the way he mic'd up the drums, the way that he approached it with musicians, the way that he made a guitar sound—I was just blown away by it all.

Tori and I rented an apartment in LA for those first couple of solo records. I wanted to be close, so I could be involved in every step of the way. I would sit sometimes ten to twelve hours a day, just watching it all unfold with some of the best players in the world, taking my ideas and adding their gift to it.

Inside, I'm still this kid from Hot Springs, Arkansas that wanted to sing, and then seemingly all of a sudden, twenty years later, I'm in the middle of this. It was a dream come true. I was so grateful because I always carried that little boy around inside of me. You can never get rid of him.

I could also never get rid of the voices in my head that reminded me constantly that I wasn't really good enough. Any situation I was in, I would metaphorically come in the back door, because I never thought I deserved to come in the front. While I had a kind of bravado on the outside, like "I'm really doing this," down in my gut I second-guessed every decision. Even after winning my first solo Grammy award, I still felt a little bit like an imposter.

Fear was also a big challenge for me during those days. When I was with The Imperials, someone else was having to make all the decisions, I could just lay back and not worry too much about anything. But when there are people on salary whose lives are affected by my choices, it made me fearful and anxious most days. Fear that it could all be gone tomorrow.

I had watched my dad shoot himself in the foot over and over again. He would get close to fulfilling a goal for the church or some other project, then he'd blow it. There was always this fear in the back of my head saying, "You're going to do that too because that's who you are and that's what you know."

But I had received a great education being with The Imperials, just watching and taking mental notes. We'd be recording an album and I'd be thinking to myself, "When I do a record, I'll do *that* differently." We'd be on the road 290 days of the year and I'd say, "I'm not going to do that!"

Of course, I wanted to write songs for my own records. It's not always an easy process, but sometimes something will happen that will spur me on to write. In the early '80s here in Nashville, there was unfortunately a frequent number of racist incidents between black and white people that would usually involve police activity and then would dominate the headlines. Horrible words would be spoken to each other. What was intriguing to me was how most everyone involved professed to be a Christian, saying they followed Jesus. Yet, I still saw prejudice.

At four o'clock in the morning I was thinking about all this and started writing, "You're my brother, you're my sister, so take me by the hand. Together we will work until He comes. There's no foe that can defeat us when we're walking side by side. As long as there is love, we will stand."

I ran upstairs and woke up Tori (which she didn't appreciate) because I was so excited. I knew that I had gotten a hold of something that was strong. She was very kind to me. "Yeah, it's really, really good," she said before falling back to sleep. I couldn't go back to sleep—I had a clear vision of what that song could be.

Division was also rampant in the Church. For instance, if a Baptist church would bring me in for a concert, none of the other kinds of churches would come. There has always been a friction between denominations, even though we're supposed to be patterning ourselves after Jesus—who drew no dividing lines. That's what we're trying to achieve, yet there's all this dissension and jealousy. I put this in the song as well.

Tori helped me finish up the lyrics and then I sat down with James Hollihan and worked on the music. We sent it out to California to our producer Bill, and he loved it, so we headed out west to cut the tracks and vocals and work on the rest of the record. Through this whole process, there are little changes here and there, but to be able to sing something I truly believed down to my gut was so fulfilling. Then radio starts playing it and it's up for Song of the Year at the

Dove Awards, you can't help but remember that four in the morning inspiration.

My first time singing that song live was in 1983 during Christian Night at Six Flags Over Texas. By the time I got to the chorus, the crowd just took over. We had four thousand people singing "You're my brother, you're my sister," and I just stopped singing. It was one of the most beautiful things I've ever heard. I stood back, and the band played for them as they sang.

Several years later, the Olympics called and wanted to use that song, but they wanted to take "Jesus" out and replace it with "love." While I believe that when I say "Jesus" I *am* saying "love," I didn't feel good about signing off on it. It just felt like gutting the core of the song and trying to pretend it wasn't really about Jesus. So, they backed away, and I never regretted it.

While I was still doing the financial juggling act to stay afloat, a family in Houston called me up and said, "We feel like God told us to buy you a bus." I was elated, of course, because renting a bus takes everything you have. This family was in commercial real estate and were doing very well that year. What a huge blessing. We found an old MCI bus for the fifty thousand dollars they sent. It wasn't brand new, but it was ours. I drove it home to Hot Springs and Bud took it down to his cabinet shop and totally built the interior. We had a bus!

There was an ongoing issue with the "facilities," however. No, we didn't have a funnel, it was a proper RV toilet, but for some reason we couldn't ever really get it completely odor-free. We used all the right chemicals, followed all the proper procedures, but still the memory lingered, if you know what I mean. I finally got so tired of the girls complaining (let's face it, guys just aren't as sensitive to those things) that I started pouring everything I could think of down that blasted toilet—bleach, household cleaner, vinegar, ammonia. Every weekend I'd try something else. I would have tried napalm if I could have gotten my hands on some. To this day Bonnie swears that she lost brain cells because of the fumes.

One of the best things about touring with my own band in my own bus is that we could stop whenever we wanted. As long as we got to the gig on time, of course. So that meant that if Tori saw a produce stand on the side of the road and yelled, "Fresh cherry cider!" we could pull over and get some. Every time we stopped to fuel the bus at a truck stop, I'd sternly announce to the band, "Make sure you get everything you need because this bus isn't stopping again for another... forty-five minutes." We ate way more truck-stop biscuits and gravy than we should have. Sometimes after a concert, if we were off the next day, we'd find an all-night bowling alley and bowl until three in the morning. My bowling name was Merle and Tori's was Trixie.

My favorite bus memory was when we were traveling through the Sequoia National Forest area. I was driving that night and I pulled the bus down off the side of the road close to a mountain stream. In the morning when the band members started waking up, we each took our steaming cup of coffee and exited the bus still in our PJs, wrapped in blankets. We could walk out across the wide flat rocks almost to the middle of the stream. We sat out there for the longest time, just talking and laughing and enjoying the sight of those unbelievably massive trees and the sound of the water.

Another time we had just played Estes Park and were driving out to California to finish work on *Walls of Glass*. We were driving through Colorado seeing all these signs saying,

"Watch for boulders" and thinking nothing of it. It was four in the morning, and all of a sudden, I heard this "WHAM!" and the bus lurched. It sounded like a shotgun had gone off right by my head. We pulled over on the side of the road and saw that we had hit a giant boulder that had rolled down onto the freeway. If we would've hit it straight on, we would've been dead. That thing was huge.

We tried to get out the door, but it wouldn't budge. The boulder had bent the door frame. Thank God the bus was still drivable. It was a Sunday, so we had no chance of finding a repair shop open to help fix our door. We got creative. When we needed to stop for food or gas, we would pop open the side window and Richard, our 5'4" bass player, would shimmy out the window. When he hit the ground, he'd grab one of those rolling ladders that semi drivers use to clean their windows, and wheel it smack up against the bus, and one by one, all eight of us would come streaming out the window. People would actually walk out of the truck stop just to watch us all get back in to the bus.

Musically, I never wanted to duplicate what I did previously, so there was a kind of progression to my next solo record that felt strange to some people. Still, we kept the same formula of great songs, great production, and hopefully great singing. Thankfully, the audience followed and even grew, in spite of *Medals* being a decidedly more synth-pop sounding project. The producer for both the *Medals* and *Russ Taff* albums was Jack Joseph Puig, who was the engineer for producer Bill Schnee on the *Walls of Glass* album.

Medals came out around the same time as Amy Grant's hugely-successful *Unguarded* album. We were on the same label at the time and were good friends. We were all so excited to see the ground Amy was breaking in the mainstream, scaling the pop charts with her single "Find A Way." There were a lot of discussions about trying to do the same kind of mainstream push with my *Medals* project through A&M Records. The talk focused on releasing "Vision" to pop radio and see what might happen. I opened for Amy on part of her "Unguarded" tour which was an incredible experience. It was my first time to be a part of a tour of such magnitude, playing to such huge audiences.

Unfortunately, the radio release never happened, so the big crossover didn't happen either. But *Medals* ended up selling a ton of records, won a Dove award, and helped grow our audience tremendously. So, it was all good.

When we started thinking about the third solo album, everyone was saying, "Just do *Medals 2*." They loved how successful it had been and wanted more of that same pop sound. That would've been easy, and probably a great career move, but I didn't want easy. And I felt like I had moved on musically. I wasn't trying to be some kind of pretentious *artiste,* but I couldn't go back and just crank out a record that fit the formula. That would feel like I was being lazy. I had been living with years of people saying, "Hey, just write another 'We Will Stand.'" I don't know how many hours I wasted trying to write "We Will Stand 2" before I realized you can't duplicate those kind of "lightning strike" moments. But now they were saying, "Hey, if you do *Medals 2* we'll get behind that in a heartbeat."

We made a conscious decision to move toward more of a rock sound for the third record. But part of that decision was me trying to find my own way, outside of the expectations of others. I was fresh out of my second stint in rehab and to say that I was feeling kind of raw and vulnerable is an understatement. The first time I heard Charlie Peacock's song "Down in the Lowlands," I was so moved. It captured my heart and I loved how it sounded musically. That song helped set the tone for the entire record. We brought Charlie in to help make the song mine and he arranged the background vocals.

Another song that laid the foundation for this third solo album came at a time when I was feeling dry as a writer. I was in Newport Beach talking to Lynn Nichols, who was my A&R guy from the label, "Lynn, I am trying to write, I really am. But when I sit down with my guitar, the thoughts just aren't coming." It was a strange, helpless feeling. Then Lynn played me "I Still Believe" by Michael Been's group The Call. It just floored me. I told Lynn, "If I could sit down right now and express what's inside me, this is the song I would write." I was standing on a balcony looking out over mountains and the ocean and I just wanted to scream out these lyrics.

In spite of all the mistakes I have made, all the hurt I have caused people, I do still believe. I never lost that. Despite all I had been through and was going through, there was a part of me that always believed I would make it out, even though I couldn't see how. I still believed in the forgiveness of sin. I still believed that He wanted me whole and free.

My favorite scripture has always been 2 Corinthians 5:17, "If any man be in Christ, he is a new creation. Old things pass away, all things become new." That's where I was. I felt like the old life was passing away and everything was becoming new.

Some of the executives at my label were concerned with how edgy this new record was sounding. Christian music hadn't yet heard anything like this from me. But one guy from the label, Loren Balman, said, "This is going to be a defining record for you. It's going to be one of those records that in ten years, you'll look back and say, 'I'm glad I made this record.'"

I made the conscious choice to let the pain of the previous year bleed into the record. I remember Tori asking, "Are you sure you want to be this honest?" I said, "Yeah, I think I do. I don't want to spend the rest of my life hiding, maybe this is how I start telling the truth." So many of the songs ended up sounding like they came straight from the Psalms, but they were a little disturbing to a lot of folks in the Christian marketplace. It wasn't a "if you're happy and you know it" kind of record. I received calls from well-intentioned friends and radio stations after hearing these songs, asking, "Um, are you and Tori okay?" I'd just smile and say, "We're fine, just walking through a few valleys over the last couple of years."

The third promise of the Twelve Promises in AA says, "We will not regret the past nor wish to shut the door on it." I wanted to use the past to help turn me into what I need to be. Joel Osteen's father, John, once told me, "Russ, God anoints your personality as well as your calling. When you are being who you are, God will bless that." I've always carried that and I'll tell young artists this a lot, "Be who you are." The *Russ Taff* project confirmed for me, that if I'm honest and real, then God will anoint that.

That's why we decided to call this album *Russ Taff,* instead of something else, because it absolutely encapsulated who I truly was at that moment in time. Some people just call it "the Grey Album" because of the black and white cover photo. We took that shot on a cliff in Malibu with a famous photographer named Phillip Dixon.

While *Medals* probably sold more, *Russ Taff* ended being one of the most critically-acclaimed records in contemporary Christian music. All these years later, I still regularly hear from people who reference that record and want to tell me how much it affected them. I'm real proud of that one. It still moves me, too.

We toured that record pretty extensively, both in and out of the US. I did several tours across Sweden, Norway, Denmark, Finland, and Germany with Andraé Crouch. We finally got to go to Australia and did a series of concerts there. Sheila Walsh invited us to perform at a benefit concert for The Prince's Trust in Royal Albert Hall, which was an unbelievable thrill. Several members of the royal family were in attendance and afterwards the other artists and I stood in a receiving line to be presented to Princess Anne. I did my best Hot Springs, Arkansas version of a formal bow as I shook her hand.

When we played the huge Greenbelt Festival in England, I was hobbling around because I had injured my knee pretty badly the day before we left the States. I'd been keeping it wrapped up in an elastic bandage to try to get the swelling down. Of course, once I walked out on stage in front of thousands of screaming Brits, and James and the band kicked into the first song, I forgot all about my bum leg. I closed the set with "I Still Believe," and got so completely wrapped up in the song that when I sang the bridge, "I'll climb this hill, upon my knees if I have to," I dramatically dropped to my knees for emphasis. And literally screamed out loud in pain. I was completely incapacitated, there was no way I could stand up, so I literally crawled all the way across the stage and managed to pull myself up onto one of the stage monitors. I never stopped singing the whole time. The crowd was going crazy, they thought they were seeing the performance of a lifetime. I finished the tour on crutches, but it was worth it.

Russ Taff fulfilled my three-record deal with Word, so after all the radio singles were worked and touring completed, I was a free agent. I had been moving in yet another musical direction lately, away from the electronic stuff and more towards a rootsy, organic sound.

I had recorded six songs that I had co-written with friends, and while there were still elements through the record that were flashes of the past records, it was definitely more acoustic, guitar driven. We shopped these tunes to all the major Christian labels. And again, they all said, "Sounds great, but…. This isn't exactly where Christian music is right now. But if you'll go back to that pop *Medals* vibe, we can definitely sell that."

Once again, it was art versus commerce. Do I just give in and give them what they want, or do I try to break out of the box and do something that excites me as an artist? It was frustrating. Fortunately, I ended up re-signing with Word Records and made *The Way Home*. The project satisfied my Americana music leanings and was very well received. It was also distributed into the pop market through A&M.

Right about this time, Mama had been diagnosed with lupus and had nearly died. She wasn't strong enough to make it to church as often as she liked, so she called one day and asked me, "Could you make me a tape of some of the old songs that we used to sing?" I knew her old record collection inside out, so song selection wasn't going to be a problem. I called in a bunch of favors from some of my friends who just happened to be some of Nashville's finest musicians, and James and I went down to his basement studio and cut five songs. It was originally just going to be for Mama, but one of the execs at Word Records ended up hearing a few of the songs and said, "Give me five more and we'll release it as an album." It was the cheapest record I ever made. We recorded *Under Their Influence* on an old Fostex B16 track recorder that would keep breaking down. We'd put it in the shop, wait for it to be fixed, then continue with the album. And it ended up winning a Grammy!

You ask musicians of a certain age which record of mine they like, and it's always this one for some reason. Guess they grew up with their Mama's record collection, too. It's the only one of my records Bill Gaither has on his iPod.

Bill invited me to be a part of the filming of their video, *Reunion: A Gospel Homecoming Celebration*. He asked me to sing "God's Unchanging Hand" from this project. The room we filmed in was filled with all the artists I had grown up with—Vestal and Howard Goodman, Jake Hess and Hovie Lister from the Statesmen, Dottie Rambo, and so many others. I was in tall cotton that day. I came in sporting my 1992 long hair and earring into a room full of much older, much more conservatively-minded folks. As I sang, they were all kind of staring at me, until halfway through the song when they started feeling the spirit.

Bill showed me the video later, and I could tell that it had been edited to make it look like they were all much more into the song from the very beginning than I remembered. Bill said, "Don't tell anybody. But for the first ninety seconds or so, you were getting a few frowns and concerned looks from people who couldn't figure out what you were doing there. But then you started singing that old song and they warmed right up to you. So, I went back and took some close-up shots from the opening prayer where everybody was smiling and nodding and edited them into the beginning of your song." That's the only time I know of where Bill doctored anything on the video shoots. Bless his heart for doing it though, I sure didn't want to watch a video of my musical heroes looking at me funny!

Shortly after this time, I had a conversation with one of the A&R directors at A&M Records and played him some of the recent tunes I had written. He said, "Have you ever thought about the country marketplace?

"No," I answered, "I haven't ever thought about that at all."

He said, "It's changing. They're signing some 'outside the box' artists these days, not just hat acts. This might work over there."

I returned to Nashville and set-up meetings with four major country labels. I didn't get any real strong interest until I got to Warner Brothers. Label President Jim Ed Norman said, "This will work. But you've got to give me some songs for radio. At least two, preferably three." I signed the deal for my *Winds of Change* project with the understanding that Warner Brothers would take my music to the country market. Their gospel label, Warner Alliance, run by Neal Joseph, would take it to the Christian marketplace.

Unfortunately, for me, I entered the country world not as an established artist with a huge track record, but rather as a rookie level, new artist. But I didn't have to swallow too much of my pride because so many of the country singers knew who I was and were so unbelievably kind to me. Garth Brooks, Tim McGraw, and Kathy Mattea all made a point of welcoming me into their world. I found out that so many country artists grew up in church and really loved Jesus. I remember sitting on the bus with Joe Diffie while on tour. He used to come see me sing in Oklahoma City before he was even a country artist. Travis Tritt and I would have long conversations about what we believed. But there were also a lot of artists I talked to that did not like the church because of what it had done to them. They were judged and condemned and decided to just walk away from it. But I was able to be myself and share my faith. Ended up having two songs hit the Top 40 in country too, so that was all new and exciting.

Warner Brothers was happy with the action of the *Winds of Change* record, so they spent 250,000 dollars on a second record. We spent four months working on the new project only to have the label decide not to release it. That little "outside the box" window apparently closed. I guess that record is still sitting on a shelf at Warner Brothers somewhere. It had some really good songs on it, too.

As you can imagine, I was left looking for direction after the Warner Brothers deal faded. *"Who wants me? Who will let me have creative liberty to do what I want?"*

Jeff Moseley had worked with me when he was at Word and was now heading up Benson Records. He expressed interest in doing a record with me. I was so thankful. He was a great champion for this new project. But halfway through the recording process, there was a corporate shake-up going on at the top and Jeff ended up leaving. So, I was stuck there. And the new person who came in did not have really know what to do with me. He didn't have Jeff's vision for the record.

That project, *Right Here, Right Now*, was probably the most difficult record I ever had to make because there were about forty different people wanting something specific from me. It transitioned from making a record that expressed me as an artist, to making a record that would please all these people who would be instrumental in making the project a success, from radio to retail.

Even still, it ended up being one of my favorite records—what we did musically and vocally, I really like it. Marcus Hummon, Becca's husband, co-wrote several of the songs with Tori and I—such an incredible writer and singer. And now knowing a bit of the story about my growing up, I hope people will appreciate the songs more. There was one particular song that Tori and I wrote right after my father's death that I still love so much called "Long Hard Road." Unfortunately, the record ended up being released with no marketing whatsoever. It was just thrown out there and then shelved. I had come full circle—from being a huge selling artist where I could do whatever I wanted, to where they're looking at me now saying, "He's very talented, but we just don't know if he'll work in our market."

Bill Gaither and I have been friends for over forty years now. He and Gloria have always been great mentors for Tori and me as far as business deals and life stuff. He and I both enjoy walking trails, so we usually have our best conversations "on the hoof." During the time just after *Right Here, Right Now*, I was sharing with him my frustrations about how the industry was changing, and we started talking about his label. He said, "You know, if you were with me, I'd let you do what you wanted to do. As long as you're having fun in there, creatively doing what inspires you, it'll be a good record." That was just beauty to my ears. I would go on to do three solo records with him.

I traveled with the Homecoming Tour for several years, and we truly became a family. Bill has never put up with egos, attitudes, or prima donnas and he's never had to—artists would kill to have a spot on that tour. So, he handpicks the singers and musicians not just based on how talented they are alone, but also on the quality of their character. He makes sure they can get along and play well with others. It makes touring so much fun because Bill does everything first class, *and* you are surrounded by first class human beings.

After I had been on the tour for a while, Mark Lowry decided to leave the Gaither Vocal Band, and I asked Bill if

I could try out for his position. It took him two weeks to make the decision to hire me, mainly because every singer in Nashville wanted to try out, too. When he finally took Tori and I to lunch at Dalts to tell me I got the job, I heaved a huge sigh of relief, then Tori hugged him and said, "Bill, if you ever need a kidney, I'll donate one of mine. But of course, I'm going to make you wait two weeks before I tell you..."

The first record I made with the Vocal Band, *Everything Good*, was a great experience—singing together with Bill and the incredible talents of Guy Penrod and David Phelps. But the second record was a nightmare for me. Bill wanted to do an a cappella project. I was horrible at it. I've never been a precise note by note singer. I'm more of a grab-'em-by-the-emotions singer. So, this was a real challenge. It's still one of Bill's favorite records, but it was all labor and no love for me. I still break out in a cold sweat when I hear one of those unbelievably difficult and complex vocal arrangements that Phelps does so brilliantly. I was not in my element at all, and finally Bill and I both agreed that it would be smart to find someone else. He brought in Marshall Hall, who ended up being just perfect. Bill kept including me in all the Homecoming tours, so I happily went back to being a solo artist.

The beautiful part of being involved with the Gaithers is that I knew that music like the back of my hand. That whole world is inside of me—the first thirteen years of my life I was indoctrinated with the music of these people I was now singing next to on the Homecoming stages. As a child, I would learn the songs of Dottie Rambo and then sing them in church. And then I was sitting next to her. Absolutely unreal. So, going from the rock music of the *Russ Taff* album to singing Southern Gospel harmonies wasn't as jarring of a transition as you might think because my musical chops were shaped on these songs and these artists.

I always understood the reality of the music business. One day you're at the top, and the next day you're not. But when it starts happening, it's not so cut and dried. You start noticing that you're not getting the phone calls to sing at the big festivals as much, radio isn't playing your music as much. Concerts start having smaller crowds and are fewer in number. Not only did it require some mental adjusting in regard to my own personal worth and value, but there was also the reality of paying the bills. I can't speak highly enough about Bill Gaither for how he's provided opportunity after opportunity for artists just like me who could use a place to land and continue to make great music.

I've been so fortunate that people still want to come see me in concert, and I've collected fans and friends from all the different musical phases of my career; from *Walls of Glass* to Gaither Homecoming videos. I have always felt a need to make sure everybody felt included and got to hear their favorite songs.

A huge honor for me came in 2012 when the Gospel Music Association honored me with a lifetime achievement segment during the Dove Awards with Jason Crabb, Donnie McClurkin, and Wess Morgan singing several of my songs during the telecast. Then in 2016 the GMA inducted me into the Gospel Music Hall of Fame. I had already been inducted as a member of The Imperials, and as a member of the Gaither Vocal Band, but this was for my solo career. What a beautiful feeling to have them recognize and honor my body of work over the years.

To hear from some of the younger artists now about how my music has influenced them is a really special joy. To meet

Bart Millard of MercyMe and have him say, "You have no idea the influence you've had on me." That's got to feel good for anybody.

I've always had this saying that at the end of my life I don't want to look back and say, "What if?" That has brought me down many different roads, but throughout I could see that God's hand was very prevalent—especially when I could I see that I went down that particular road for that one particular person I was meant to connect with.

But it's all definitely changed how I define success. Is it that you've done the same thing over and over and made a lot of money? Or is it being able to follow a dream and allow creativity to take you into all kinds of areas? To me, it's been the latter. I feel like I have been successful. It would be great to have the bank account of some of my peers, but as I look back over my career, I'm just so grateful for the things He's allowed me to do and places He allowed me to go. Tori and I have seen a lot of the world together. She's dragged me through museums, art galleries, and historic sites all over Europe, Australia, South Africa, and South America. We've had a ball.

After forty-some years of doing this, who knows how much longer God will allow me stay out here. I hope *a lot* longer.

WE WILL STAND

Sometimes it's hard for me to understand
Why we pull away from each other so easily
Even though we're all walking the same road
Yet we build dividing walls between our brothers and ourselves

But I, I don't care what label you may wear
If you believe in Jesus you belong with me
The bond we share is all I care to see

And we can change this world forever
If you will join with me, join and sing

Oh you're my brother, you're my sister
So take me by the hand
Together we will work until He comes
There's no foe that can defeat us
When we're walking side by side
As long as there is love we will stand

The day will come when we will be as one
And with a mighty voice together
We will proclaim that Jesus, Jesus is King
And it will echo through the earth
It will shake the nations and the world will see, see that

You're my brother, you're my sister
So take me by the hand
Together we will work until He comes
There's no foe that can defeat us
When we're walking side by side
As long as there is love we will stand

(words by Russ & Tori Taff)

Joseph Layton Taff and
Annie Mae Johnson in
Hot Springs, Arkansas,
around 1943.

Dad (wavy hair courtesy
of Lucky Tiger hair tonic)
holding me in Steelville,
Missouri, where I was born.

Earl Lee and me, only 16
months apart. Got that
protective big-brother arm
around him even then.

Singing at a wedding,
Eastside Tabernacle,
Farmersville, CA. I was about
9, and that microphone
was as big as my head.

Taff family, L to R: Marvin, Dad,
Russ, Mom, Bill, Earl, Danny

Mom and my aunts,
The Johnson Sisters, L
to R: Joyce, Maudin,
Bertha, Ann, Elsie

Mom taught me how
to play guitar.

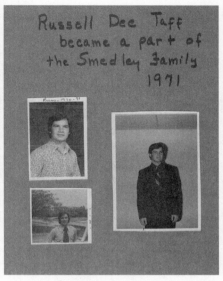

Jesus Movement, early
70's, singing with my
band, the Sounds of Joy.

From Mama June's scrapbook.

Sounds of Joy performing at Hot Springs High
school assembly— Tori was in the audience.

The cheerleader.

Dating in the early 70's. (Note— Russ is showing a lot of cleavage for a gospel singer.)

Tori's high school prom, 1974.

The Timm family, L to R: Joel, Matt, Tori, Jonathan, Carolyn, Liz (Note—I have no idea why Liz and I were dressed as sailors.)

L to R: Kim Smedley, my best man Bud Smedley, Mama
June, Russ, Tori the child bride, Earl, Stuart Smedley.

Our wedding, Oct. 31, 1976.
(Not pictured— honeymoon
trick or treaters.)

You may kiss your bride.

Singing with the Imperials,
matching suit version.

Early publicity shot—
Jim Murray, Russ, Dave
Will (is that a jumpsuit?),
Armond Morales

The Imps with our favorite
producer, Michael Omartian.

Sharp dressed men.

Amazing four-part harmony
and a questionable skinny tie.

'Medals' tour dates

Mama June's backstage passes.

Playing air guitar with James 'Dr. J' Hollihan.

Touring Europe with the
best band in gospel music.

His and her mullets
in Amsterdam.

In South Africa with
World Vision.

Rockin' the house with the
late, great Jackie Street.

Collecting hardware.

Being presented to Princess
Anne after a concert for
the Prince's Trust at the
Royal Albert Hall.

Best of times, worst of times.

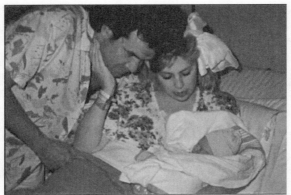

Maddie Rose is born—
we're a family!

Charlotte loving Jesus.

Cool moms—Amy
Grant and Sarah, Tori
and Maddie Rose at a
Gaither Artist Retreat.

My best girls.

My Homecoming friends,
Alaskan cruise.

I have no idea what Bill
Gaither just said to me, but
apparently it was pretty funny.

Best vacation of our lives—
a Mediterranean cruise
with Bill and Gloria.

That time the Gaither Vocal
Band performed at the Sydney
Opera House in Australia…

Our hearts.

Tori, Maddie Rose and Charlotte
in a Savannah courtyard.

Russ and Charlo looking for
puffins in the Faroe Islands.

Same boat, different daughter.

Zach Glickman, our beloved manager
(and Jewish mother) for 30 years.

Mercy me, Bart came to the Buckle!

A publicity shot from my
brief foray into country
music. Couldn't fit a cowboy
hat over all that hair.

Modeling headshot.

Second chance at Imperials
reunion— thanks, Dan!

Walking the red carpet
with my best girls
to receive a Lifetime
Achievement recognition
at the GMA Dove Awards.

'Birthday baseball'
from Santa Fe, signed
by the therapists.

Russ and Tori's Bell Buckle
Weekend meet and greet
in our front yard.

Concert at the Bell
Buckle Banquet Hall.

So honored to be a
part of that Unbroken
Circle-- what a thrill!

"I Still Believe" documentary premiere at the Franklin Theater: God's mercy and grace were on full display, and we have never felt so loved in our lives. L to R: Amy Grant, Russ, Steven Curtis Chapman, Mary Beth Chapman, Tori.

Grateful.

Q & A session following the film with director Rick Altizer.

SEVEN

UNCOVERING THE RUBBLE

The Christian market has been so cruel to some of its people who have fallen. Naturally, I didn't want to make my story public in the middle of it still being written. I didn't want to have to explain it all while I was in the process of recovery and working to get my life back. I didn't want to be a poster child for alcoholics in the Christian marketplace. I also didn't want to destroy my career.

My grown-up way of hiding was to create a persona that was a sort of mask I could wear, a fashioning of the person people wanted to see. I would hold the mask up and people would love it. But it felt like nobody really loved *me*, because nobody knew me. I still had a longing for acceptance inside of me. I kept hoping that hole would be filled up by the next accomplishment or award. It never worked, of course. It was awful for good things to happen to me when I didn't feel worthy. I couldn't trust it. If I would try to hang onto it and it goes away, I would feel just devastated. I lived most of my life holding this image up and dying on the inside.

> Tori: *He also had a mask he would wear around me.*
> *It was the mask of a happy husband who loves*
> *his wife.*
> Russ: *I thought if I could make you happy, then every-*
> *thing would be good.*

TORI

But as the disease progressed, it started going away. He didn't have the energy to keep up the happy husband mask anymore, even though he still had the "successful Christian artist" mask for everyone else.

A therapist told us once that an addict doesn't know what normal is or what happy feels like, so they guess at it. They look at other people that they think are happy or normal and try to act like they do. There was a lot of that early on. Then that started going away to where he'd come home and not even try to put in any effort, simply disappearing further down that hole of more addiction and depression.

But now we can understand why it was so exhausting for Russ to keep up all those masks because he was trying with all his might to keep the trauma at bay, the memories, the residual pain. So, with the exhaustion would come frustration and anger over the fact that none of his efforts or accolades were making him feel any better.

RUSS

I saw that I was doing to Tori what my dad had did to me. It broke my heart that I was traumatizing her the way my dad traumatized me. She was wary and walking on eggshells, trying to figure out what I was going to do next. And that made the shame even more intense.

I was left crying out to God, "Where are you?" Through all the years of the worst pain and struggle, the only thing that would bring me up just a little bit was when I would have an encounter with Jesus—him showing up in places he shouldn't have shown up. Like a taste of sweet water on a dry tongue. It was almost like he was just saying, "This is what you're looking for, follow me." And I would say, "I don't know how!" I didn't feel I deserved that love.

I would shout at God, "All I ever wanted to do was sing for you!" I was thinking that if I did that, then He would make me happy. But what he was trying to do was heal me. I was looking for a quick fix, a miracle. But what he wanted to do would take years.

On stage, I had always presented the message that we all struggle. I'd share things from stage about how I "overcame," but I would do it in a way that everybody could understand, so it was never specific to alcohol. It left some people wondering if our marriage was okay or if I was getting a divorce. We are such curious creatures. I always knew I did not want to fight my battles in the public eye. I wanted to fight my battle with addiction surrounded by a group of people that understood what I was walking through.

I had been attacked before, mostly by people who were jealous of my success and wanted to tear me down. One was an evangelist who told lies about me because I wouldn't leave my job and go with him. I also had a couple other Christian artists spread some false rumors over the years. Ironically, one of them was about seeing me coming out of a hotel room with a blonde—it was Tori! So, I had reason to be concerned that if I gave anyone any ammunition by revealing my battle with alcoholism that we'd just be pouring gas on a potential career-ending fire.

That's what made the night we recorded the *Timeless* live DVD such a horrific event.

EIGHT

EXPOSED AND ASHAMED

I t was going to be an incredible night celebrating some of the best music of the previous twenty years in Christian music. It was called *Timeless* and would be a live CD and DVD recorded one evening in 2007. I'd be on stage with a dozen or so artists who had done well over the past years. We all knew each other, so it was a bit of a homecoming event for us. Each artist would step out and sing a couple of their biggest hits, and then the night would end with me joining the guys from The Imperials to sing "Praise the Lord" for the finale of the night. I hadn't sung together with them for years.

This would also be the first time that I would be absolutely drunk on stage. I picked a doozy of a night to do that, too, since it was being filmed in front of a packed house of friends and half of the music industry. But the timing of this event could not have been any worse for me personally, as my mother had just died.

When Dad died it was as if there was nothing left to hold in this rage that I felt toward him. I don't know why I could hold in the rage while he was alive, maybe out of respect. But it was out the window when he died, and I couldn't contain myself. I sat at the funeral as a son who loved his daddy. But I was also a son who hated his daddy for what he did to me and my brothers. After almost eleven years of sobriety, I relapsed. I didn't have any tools to know what to do with all the pain. All I knew was that I hurt so bad, and I just wanted it to go away. It makes sense that a person would want intense pain to go away, doesn't it? The problem is that alcoholics do it in the one way that's guaranteed to create more pain. Then my loved ones staged the intervention, I went to treatment, and got sober again.

In June of 2000, my baby brother Earl died from addiction at age forty-five. The doctor said that his liver had basically exploded, and that he had to have known that he was dying for weeks before he actually did. But he didn't tell anyone, and he didn't go to the hospital. My survivor's guilt was overwhelming. What if I had insisted that Earl stay in Arkansas with me all those years ago? What if I had gone back to California with the family and tried to protect him— would his life have turned out differently? It knocked my legs out from under me, and when I got back from his funeral, I had a couple of nights where I tried to drink those feelings away again. But I quickly pulled myself back together and confessed to Tori and my AA sponsor. I got back on track, doubling up on my meetings until I was on solid ground.

But then when Mama died, after another long stretch of sobriety, all those feelings thundered back, and the wheels came off for good. Another relapse. It just felt like loss after loss after loss—each one stirring up memories that were becoming increasingly hard to shove back down. I sat at her funeral thinking, "Why didn't you protect us, Mama?" I thought about how she taught me how to sing and play guitar, which is my life, but "Why didn't you get us out of the house?" There was so much craziness going on in my head. Love and anger were equally fierce and equally valid. I flew home from Mama's funeral knowing that I had broken Tori's heart one more time. I told her I had gotten myself together now and stopped, but I don't think she truly believed me. Because I was lying.

The day came for the video shoot, and I had a little bit to drink before we did sound check, but everything went fine. It was during the three-hour period between then and the start of the concert where I had a little more. And a little more. Because when I would drink, I didn't hate Mama as bad. I wouldn't be as angry at her. I wouldn't hurt as much.

I don't even remember walking out on the stage.

TORI

This was the beginning of one of the worst experiences of my life.

Leading up to the night of the *Timeless* event, I had seen Russ acting weird. I was in constant contact with my therapist because Russ was obviously spiraling out of control. It was like he just couldn't stay sober, even though he had been to treatment twice already. He was gone a lot, he was angry, he was showing up at therapy sessions and walking out in the middle of them. We were in a whole 'nother level of pain, and a whole 'nother level of destruction—self-destruction. He wasn't fading away anymore. He was cutting his own throat. The memories that he had shoved down, were now flooding back to the point that he couldn't suppress them. He was self-medicating hard to get numb as much as possible.

When the night of the concert came around, I was already living in a guarded camp with him emotionally. He was so volatile and the counselor and I had been trying to calm him down, trying to coax him out into the open, so we could get him someplace safe.

I stayed home that night which was a little unusual. We had a new gas grill that was being delivered that evening, so that gave me a good excuse to stay home. But at this point, I was so traumatized and angry myself, I didn't feel like seeing him on stage or hear him talking about God, even if my gut knew that in whatever shape he was in that was the one real part of him. If he lied to me about everything else, that part was real. I also didn't want to sit in the audience and listen to everybody talk about that voice and how wonderful he was.

But him going on stage drunk was simply unimaginable.

Dan Posthuma, producer of the Timeless event

My wife Sarah and I have had a great relationship with Russ and Tori for years. I had started working with Russ back in the early '80s, helping with his live show, and then on several of his big albums from the label side. I just fell in love with him and Tori—their spirits, their heart for God, and their love for music.

Russ was with us that afternoon for rehearsal. He had shared some old stories about his career and why certain songs were meaningful to him. In retrospect, I should have been more aware of the pain involved for Russ in telling some of these old stories. And the other artists were just so excited to have him there and were paying him a lot of extravagant compliments. There was a lot of attention being focused on him, and I know Russ well enough that I knew it was a challenge for him. But I didn't realize how vulnerable he would be as a result. It blindsided both of us, obviously.

Chonda Pierce, host of the Timeless event

I was going to introduce Russ, we would chat a little bit because we were pals and everybody knew that, so they thought they'd get some funny stuff out of us. He was a preacher's kid, and I was a preacher's kid, so we were going to talk about funny things that happened in services as preachers' kids. The rehearsal went well. We had a little script we were supposed to follow, but of course, I never follow it. We veered off and had funny ideas and stories. So backstage, we're like, "Okay, that worked out great. Here's what I'm going to say. Okay. Then I'll say this, and then you say this, and then that'll lead you to be able to tell this story."

Dan Posthuma

We had all agreed to meet for prayer about an hour before we started. I looked around and Russ was gone. He was obviously an important part of the show since we had planned the climax to be a moment where Russ would sing with his old group. During rehearsal, Russ seemed excited to be singing with those guys again.

I wasn't too concerned. I've worked with Russ for many, many years and I know something about his sense of timing in terms of sometimes showing up a little late for rehearsals and things like that. I thought, "He's just going and taking a little rest, resting his voice before things start."

RUSS TAFF AND TORI TAFF

About five minutes before we took the stage, Russ came running in, said hello and took his place. Our emcee, Chonda Pierce, started her conversation with Russ. I had a feeling that things weren't exactly right—he was moving around a little bit too much.

Chonda Pierce

When I introduced him, I could immediately smell him on his way to the stage. It was a very familiar smell to me. But my first thought was, one, we're in the middle of this taping and two, all of these people are watching. You can splice and edit here and there, but all of these people in the audience watching are going to know of his great struggle.

My mind was racing, going, "How do I get him out of this? And how's he going to sing the next song?" I was not as familiar with how he might have pulled this off down through the years, or if he's even *had* to pull this off in public before. I took his hand and stood there by him. I wanted so badly to not let anybody know his secret that he wasn't ready to let know. Then there was a great panic that came over me. At that particular time, I had no idea that a few years from then, I would be having to deal with the same kind of horrible situation in my own home. I so badly wanted to be clever enough and funny enough that people would not know what I knew, what I could smell, what I could sense, and what I could see of him staggering. I thought about, "What if I just tackled him," or, "What if he just tripped and we said he was having a stroke or something." You start thinking of all these scenarios of how we could help salvage him. Not salvage the moment, or the video, but how do we salvage *him*, so that he can save face and not be so humiliated. But there comes a time when it becomes so blatant, that there's nothing you can do but just hold on in the middle of it.

I saw a man who was in great pain. That pain got the best of him that day, and he had to go medicate it. That, to me, is the thing you sense first. You see it in their eyes. He had this look of not just panic because "I can't remember what the words are" or "what I'm supposed to say next," but after the fog of alcohol and the addiction is scraped away, deep down in those eyes, there's a great pain back there. It's really sad. Oh, that we could all see that. You would step over the homeless a lot differently. You'd be a lot more merciful for the guy that comes into church and doesn't dress like you. Oh, that we could all see past addiction to see why it's really there. It's sad. It comes with a great burden and a great price.

Dan Posthuma

I started to wonder if he was feeling alright. But it's hard to tell with Russ because he has this rock and roll swagger about him. He has a voice that can cut through steel, but his charm is when he starts talking, you just fall in love with him. He has such a great heart of gold.

My son, who was up in the balcony, texted me and said, "I think Russ is drunk." I dismissed that immediately. I knew Russ had had some alcohol issues in the past, a long time ago, but didn't think that was the situation here.

The more I watched him, I thought, "Whatever is happening I need to get this guy off stage as quickly as possible. For his own good and for the good of all the rest of the artists in the show." There wasn't a convenient way to do that other than while somebody else was singing, so I just walked on stage and tapped him on the shoulder. I said, "Russ, follow me." He gave me a look of, "What's happening here?" but he came with me. We walked backstage, and it didn't take one minute before I immediately knew what the problem was. My son had been right—he was quite intoxicated.

Russ started weeping, apologizing, and said, "Dan I'm so sorry, I don't know how this happened, I don't know what went wrong, I'm so sorry."

"Russ just sit down," I said, "take a deep breath and we'll see what we need to do here."

"Let me back on that stage," he pleaded. "I want to get back there, I want to sing. I haven't sung with those Imperials guys for years, this is my big opportunity, all my friends are out there in the seats. I want to do this."

"Russ, I don't think that's a good idea," I replied.

"But, 'Praise the Lord,' you're going to let me sing that. That's how we're going to end this concert, 'Praise the Lord.' You're going to let me sing that, aren't you?"

"Russ," I said, "I think you just need to sit here and rest. We need to find a way to get you home." That's when he totally lost it. It was hard to watch because I have so much love for this man.

I knew he couldn't get back on that stage. That wouldn't be fair to him, and it certainly wouldn't be fair to all the other artists that were involved. He argued and argued as best he could. He pleaded, he got angry, then he got solemn—he was so intoxicated he couldn't continue any of that for very long.

Thankfully, Sarah was back there with me, and she said, "Russ, give me your car keys." He said, "No, no, I'm fine. I can drive home." She answered, "No, you can't. Give me your car keys." He eventually did. Sarah found Russ' daughter in the audience and drove them home.

It was obviously a very troubling and painful experience, mostly for Russ, but for those of us who love him as well. And it put a big hole in the show, and disappointed many, many people. The concert was kind of built around the reunion of those two entities, The Imperials and Russ.

After the concert—which was very successful at many levels, even without the magic moment at the end—we were all shaken. We had heard and seen what had happened with Russ. All the artists were talking about it backstage. And then we stopped and prayed for him.

Some of the artists were very gracious, saying "He obviously has a problem. And we want to do everything we can to help." And a few of the other artists said, "He obviously has a problem, and he shouldn't have put us in that position. He shouldn't have done that to the show." I remember thinking, *both of those things are right*. More than anything, though, you could sense the care, love, and concern in the room that night.

Somebody said, "We need to keep this to ourselves. We don't want to hurt our brother in this. He's obviously hurting enough. We need to love him through this, and pray him through this, and keep quiet about it. This is a family matter."

Everybody agreed.

Bonnie Keen, Tori's best friend and member of First Call

Some might call what happened that night the end of his career, marriage, and family. I believe it was the only chance Russ had for a new beginning. Time kind of stopped for all of us.

His private struggle refused to be hidden one minute longer. He was a drowning man. He was going down and gasping for air.

I saw my big brother begging for a lifeline. Like watching a hemorrhaging child plead for a tourniquet.

In hindsight, I wonder if something about this group of friends made it a strange sort of safe place for Russ to fall apart. I'd like to think so.

Chonda Pierce

Down through the next few years, I would see Bonnie Keen, Bryan Duncan, or somebody else from that night, and it was like we all had a secret. *Anybody heard from Russ? How's Russ doing?* Nobody said a word. There's a beautiful hidden comradery for people who walk a road that no one understands. We are co-conspirators to all of our secrets. Is that a good thing? Not always. Sometimes people's secrets need to be found out, so they can't hide behind them anymore. But some secrets are for no one to know until they're ready to reveal them.

Dan Posthuma

I got a call from Tori later that night. She was shaken. She said, "I'm not sure Russ is going make it through this." I remember thinking, if anybody could pull this off, Tori can. She loves this man deeply, and she's a strong, strong woman.

TORI

The first sign that something was wrong was when I heard a car pull into the driveway while I was struggling to get the new grill put together. Maddie Rose and her friend walked in the front door, home from the concert way too early.

"What are you doing back?"

Maddie Rose said, "I don't know. Dad was feeling bad or weird or something. I think he's medicated—some kind of medication that made him sleepy or something. We had a designated driver bring us home." Dan's wife, Sarah, had driven them home.

I said, "What?" and my heart started racing, my whole body had a complete physical response. A clutch of fear that is indescribable. Everything in me is going *no, no, no.*

My mind starting whirling—*what did he do*?

I walked in where Russ was, and he was in a fog. I said, "What the hell is going on?" There was this feeling of, *this can't be happening.*

Russ wouldn't even look at me. "I don't know…"

This was the first time that I had seen him so obviously impaired. That may sound weird coming from someone who had known for decades she was married to an alcoholic, but I hadn't ever had to physically deal with a falling down drunk husband before—until that night. Though his secret drinking was crazy-making in and of itself, I had always been grateful that I didn't have years' worth of horrible pictures in my head, like Russ had of his father. I always thought that was one of the main reasons I had been able to stay and fight for the marriage. So, I can't emphasize enough the shock of actually seeing him as I had pictured his dad had been. I had a drunk Russ standing right in front of me, thick-tongued and blank. Unrecognizable.

I immediately thought about our beloved friend, Dan, and how Russ had probably just ruined Dan's big night. I led Russ straight into our bedroom and he fell into our bed. I kept trying to piece together what had happened. "You were fine when you left here, when did you drink? Did you go on stage like this?" That's when the anger came. He was getting mad at me for freaking out so much and didn't want to talk to me. I had so much stress adrenaline coursing through my body I felt like I was levitating.

"Russ, do not take one foot out of this bedroom. I mean it. *Do not move.*" I was hyper-aware that Maddie and her friend were still wandering around the house and Charlotte was upstairs in her room. I shut the bedroom door behind me, arranged my face into something resembling a smile and walked into the kitchen where the girls were. In what I hoped was a normal mom voice I asked, "Want some brownies?"

I had known ever since his mom had died that Russ in trouble and been trying to get him help. But this was the line that had never been crossed, this was the final breaking point. He had never walked out on stage drunk in front of an audience of his peers and God and everyone. It struck such fear in my heart because I knew this was the last boundary—Russ was in freefall. If this happened, then I thought we lost him.

I called Dan. I was horrified and kept apologizing. I mean, I wasn't apologizing for me. I was apologizing that this happened to Dan. And even though I had my black belt in Al-Anon, there was still a part of me that thought if I'd gone with him maybe this wouldn't have happened. Even though I knew I couldn't keep him from drinking—we were decades into that realization—maybe I could've stopped him from going on stage. But it had to happen, as ugly and horrifying as it was.

RUSS

I was thinking, *I've destroyed myself. I've destroyed Tori. I'm destroying my kids. And now my career. And Tori's probably going to leave me. She's had enough.* Not only was I dealing with Mama's death, but now I was dealing with me and what I have done. I just wanted to run and go someplace where nobody knew where I was and start a new life.

TORI

I walked back in the bedroom. Russ was trying to get out of the bed, like he was going somewhere. He said, "I need to go."

I was furious, but deadly calm. "You're not going anywhere. Just get back in bed and go to sleep, we'll talk in the morning." He sat on the edge of the bed with his head hanging down. And then he got up and started to walk toward the kitchen.

I grabbed him by the arm, "Oh no you don't," and literally pushed him back into the bedroom and onto the bed. He wasn't fighting me, but he had this ridiculous look of drunken surprise and indignation on his face, like, "What? Have I somehow offended you?" Afterwards, he decided he was going to get in the car and leave.

Of course, I wasn't going to allow that to happen. "Where are your keys?" I asked. He tried to hide that he had them in his hand. "You're not leaving this room. And you're definitely not driving the car!"

"I am too," he insisted. I grabbed at the keys with both hands. He wasn't swinging at me, but he was resisting me. This was the most physical confrontation we've ever had. We're not even yellers and shouters, much less pushers and shovers. Another line crossed. But I was bound and determined that I would do whatever it took to keep this man from leaving the bedroom and walking out where the girls were. While he was struggling to step away from me, I made a grab for the keys and as I yanked them out of his hand, the car key raked across his forehead. A thin line of blood went all the way up to his hairline, like a cat scratch. I knew it wasn't a serious wound, but I absolutely could not believe I drew blood.

Russ looked at me like he was in shock, and I shoved him backwards down into a chair. I felt like I was watching a bad movie. Part of me wanted to fall down on my knees and plead with him to turn back into Russ again. Instead, I leaned over him, and got nose to nose, right up in his face. I won't repeat exactly what I said, but was along the lines of, "If you walk out of this room, and my children see you like this, I will *end you*." And I meant it.

Russ slumped down into the chair. I was shaking uncontrollably, but I took a deep breath, squared my shoulders, and walked into the kitchen to serve the brownies. When I went back to check on him about ten minutes later, he was gone. Russ had a spare car key and had climbed out the bedroom window. I didn't know he did this until I heard the car drive away. I had no idea where he might head, or if he could even keep the car on the road in the shape he was in.

RUSS

I just wanted to get away and drink until I passed out, and drink until I passed out, and drink until I passed out. That's the way my dad used to do it. I knew if I sobered up, the pain and reality of what I had done was going to be so overwhelming, I would not be able to function. It's unbearable to look at somebody that you love and realize you just stuck a knife in them—I couldn't live with that. I could not cope.

TORI

I was trying so hard to protect the girls from Russ' disease, so they wouldn't have to be affected by it like he had. They knew he was an alcoholic and that he went to meetings, but they had never directly experienced anything like this. When I realized Russ was gone, I immediately called his phone, but he wouldn't pick up. So, began a long night of trying to find him. In the middle of my first flurry of phone calls, Maddie Rose walked into my room. "What's wrong with Daddy and where did he go?" I gave up the pretense. I looked her in the eye and said, "Honey, we are going to be alright, but your dad's in trouble right now." She said, "How are we going to find him?"

Knowing the dynamics of Russ' home, and how his mother turned to him to fill her emotional needs, I was determined to deal with my marital issues completely apart from the girls. *I'm the adult here. That's not their job.* We never lied to them, we made sure to keep our explanations about addiction age-appropriate, and obviously, didn't share too many details. I didn't want them to ever feel responsible for either one of us. But that night I was afraid that Russ was going to hurt himself. Maddie Rose could tell how scared I was, and she stayed with me in the kitchen all night while I was trying to find Russ.

Maddie Rose was cold and angry at her dad, and I knew that was because she didn't want to feel vulnerable and afraid for him. Sometimes anger feels like strength. I downplayed the situation to Charlotte, but I caught her glancing at me sharply, trying to read my face. She mainly stayed in her room and would come down occasionally and check on me. These are the classic roles that children take on in alcoholic homes, the ones that I somehow thought we could successfully avoid. It made me heartsick.

The doctors had told me before that even at his worst, Russ wasn't actively suicidal—that's just not in him. He's self-destructive, yes, but I'd never worried about him blowing his head off or something…until that night. Because what had happened was so huge and he had crossed that final line, I knew he was out of his mind, and I couldn't fathom what he was capable of doing. That whole night is a blur. I spent most of it with my determined little shadow Maddie Rose in the kitchen with me, while her friend slept upstairs.

I thought he might possibly head to our lake house. I called the local police there and they went out to check. They called me back and said, "It doesn't appear that anybody has been at the house." Then I got the idea to start tracking his credit card. I called the credit company, and they helped me track him to a hotel about fifty miles away in Dickson. I called the hotel and probably sounding like a crazy person, said, "Look, you don't know me. But my husband is an alcoholic and he's in a relapse. His mother just died, and I have real concerns that he might harm himself." And I'll never forget, because that lady was like, "Oh, honey…been there. Hang tight, let me see what I can do." I love the South. But by the time we zeroed in, he was gone.

RUSS

I didn't know where I was going that night. There were times when I would just let go of the steering wheel, just to see how long it would take me to veer off. I didn't want to kill myself, but it sure crossed my mind because I hated myself so much.

TORI

I finally tracked him to a Holiday Inn Express in Lebanon, which was nearly one hundred miles from the first hotel in Dickson. I called Becca Stevens. She and another friend, Dr. John Shaw, knew about Russ' mom's death and some of what had been going on with him. They told me to stay there and offered to go find Russ and bring him home. I think they were concerned for what I'd find.

About two hours later, they walked through the front door. Russ still had alcohol in him, but he wasn't drunk. I was filled with the most intense wave of relief I've ever experienced. And I also wanted to take a meat cleaver to him.

RUSS

I cried all the way home because I was starting to sober up. And I knew that if I was going home, I couldn't drink anymore which meant the weight of everything I had done would be hitting me right in the face. I didn't know if I could handle that. Also, at this point, I knew Tori was done. I was already thinking I would probably be moving out into one of those single dad apartments soon. There was no way the marriage was going to survive this one.

But I hung my life on Tori. She was the only source of love and sanity I had left. And if I lost grip of her, I would just be floating out in space somewhere, totally abandoned and alone. The thought of her leaving terrified me. But the thought of living every day with her anger and disappointment scared me, as well. I felt trapped.

The next day I met with Walt Quinn, an old friend and AA buddy. Something happened in me during our long conversation—Walt's patient but firm "program talk." I reluctantly decided that with God's help, I wouldn't give up just yet. I would keep working to do whatever it took to get my life back and keep our marriage together.

So, I went back home, and Tori and I sat down with the girls. I had some explaining to do.

TORI

The thing about addiction is that there's a very thin line between realizing you have a problem and feeling sorry for yourself. I used to say that self-pity was the poison at the root of Russ' family tree. It's very easy to blame everyone and everything else for the mess you're in, and that is guaranteed to keep you drunk. Self-pity says, "Nobody understands me or knows the pain that I've been through."

My concern was that if our conversation with the girls turned into being "poor Daddy and his horrible childhood," I just couldn't bear it. But instead, Russ was very calm and focused, and he made it about them. He said, "Girls, you know that Daddy Joe had the disease of alcoholism. I told you how he drove everyone away and died alone in a hospital room mad at everybody. Well, I have that same disease and I don't want to do that. So, I'm going to go to a place where they will work with me and teach me how to figure out what's going on and why I can't get well. It isn't far away, so you can come see me. But I need to do this because you deserve it." Thankfully, the girls accepted it exactly as he put it out. He spoke at the level they understood, and he went off to Cumberland Heights again.

This was the third treatment, so I wasn't exactly full of hope going in. This was literally the last call.

Maddie Rose Taff, daughter

After I got home from the *Timeless* event, apparently Dad was passed out in the house and Mom was trying to wake him up and get him stable. I wasn't fully aware of what was going on, but the whole concert thing had been so odd, I knew something was happening. The way I dealt with a lot of this back then is that I would go walking around the neighborhood. So, I just started walking down the side of our street towards the arboretum. The next thing I looked up and Dad is driving past me in his car, really fast. He made eye contact, but it was like he looked right through me and kept on driving. Then he just disappeared. When he finally came home, things were so intense. I locked myself in my room and was throwing things against the wall because I was so mad. That's the last thing I remember, until he sat us down and said he was going away to a treatment center. My mother was obviously very protective of us and scared, but she was also left with trying to sort out this giant emergency we were all in the middle of. She spent a lot of time holed up in her room on the phone trying to put out fires, so I didn't see a lot of her. My sister was holed up in her room doing computer stuff. We all just kind of isolated. Nobody really knew what to do.

There's a whole year I don't remember. I have little bits of fuzzy memory here and there. That's what trauma does—it blocks the brain from memories that are too painful for the heart to handle. But I was definitely lost for quite a few years. I acted out, put myself in some bad situations. And to this day, I'm not exactly sure why. But it had a scarring effect on me for sure.

Charlotte Taff, daughter

Growing up, it wasn't the addiction of alcohol that affected us because we never saw that—it was smoking. It was the same kind of behavior, sneaking and hiding and saying he'll quit, but he doesn't. We thought it was the worst thing in the world, so we would nag at him and say, "Dad, please don't smoke." And he'd respond, "I'm sorry, girls. It's really hard for me to quit this, but I promise I'll try."

Mom sheltered me a lot from the main stuff that happened, like when Dad relapsed, and we couldn't find him—I didn't really know that was happening. I was so mad about that when I found out later because I'm a part of this family too and wanted to help any way I could. I felt like they had shut me out because I was the youngest. As I grew older, I started to realize the extent of what had happened, how horrible it could have been. I remember Mom telling me later, when I was an adult, that when it was at its worst she had been seriously thinking about moving us to Arkansas to live with my mom's family. We weren't sure what would happen to Dad.

There are parts of him that I really didn't see a lot of when I was a kid. Like, happiness. Once, years after all of this, we were going to Gaither Family Fest, and Dad had a new medication for his depression. He was so happy, motivated to do anything and everything. I turned to Mom, and said, "I've never seen dad like this before." She said, "This is what he was like before everything had affected him so much."

I dealt with all of this mostly in seclusion—with my games and videos, veering off to the side, not wanting to deal with all the family drama. In a way, that stunted me in dealing with certain situations. I think I was kind of the lost child, trying to stay out of everybody's way and not further rock the boat. I didn't really feel like I had a voice. To this day, confrontation of any kind is still a huge challenge for me. When I was eighteen, I was diagnosed with anxiety and started taking medication for it. Having Mom and Dad be so open about what they've gone through has taught me how to not be afraid to ask for help. It has really helped me get out of my shell and be more of the person I want to be.

RUSS

I can look back now and say that horrible night was one of the most merciful things that ever happened to me. It shocked me into getting very real and very honest. It made me see that the trauma of my childhood was never going to go away and would keep me a prisoner until I could get help and finally deal with it.

It's still difficult for me to drive by that church where the *Timeless* concert was held, even after all these years. It was so unspeakably humiliating to do that in front of my friends and industry people, but also to do that to Dan and the production company that had spent so much money and time to put it all together. But sometimes the greatest tragedies can become the most important turning points in our lives—a start of something brand new, and a new level of grace that you've never known.

I'm also so overwhelmingly grateful for how the artists involved that night responded. They could have destroyed me, but instead, they chose to love me. Gloria Gaither has always told me, "I've never seen artists pull together to cover someone and help someone like they did with you." They saw the hurt and the pain. They didn't gossip, they didn't trash me. They all wanted me to get well. I fully expected to start getting negative phone calls from promoters and pastors because the word had gotten out. I've seen other artists go through things and how this town can be very cruel. But nobody said a word.

TORI

Russ won't say this, but I will. At his worst, at his most sick, at the point where he hated himself the most, he still consistently showed mercy to others. He consistently was the one reaching out a hand. He consistently was the one cheerleading from the side. And it was real. Every person that was there that night had experienced some part of that. Believe me, I'm not saying out of all the alcoholics in the world he wins "alcoholic of the year." At his worst, he's capable of what every alcoholic is capable of. But all those years when he was telling himself that he was worthless, he was making a whole lot of people feel worthy. And he wasn't faking it, he wasn't flattering them, he meant it. And that is what was being returned to him.

RUSS

With my dad, I saw how everything in his life was always somebody else's fault. One of his relapses he blamed on me when I was sixteen because I dented his car. As I turned into a man, I said I will never do that. I will take responsibility for what I've done and not blame anybody else. I had to do that with this situation. When people would ask me questions, I told them what happened.

TORI

The alcoholic has to lie to stay alive. In recovery, the man that was walking out of the darkness decided to speak to truth. The only reason we're still married is because there was never once in the decades of our marriage when he said, "Well, if you had just done this or not done that, maybe I wouldn't drink." And when I was screaming my accusations at him in the therapist's office, he'd look me right in the eye and say, "I did it, and I'm sorry." It didn't make me feel better, but it gave us something to build on.

RUSS

She saw somebody trying to stop hiding. Trying to be the person I wanted to be. God cannot change us if we don't acknowledge the problem and accept responsibility. I believe healing comes when the Holy Spirit shines light on these dark areas, and you're able to say, "Yes, I did that, and I can't live with it. You've got to help me deal with that."

I'm a living testimony of what the power of Christ can do in a person's life. But you have to stay consistent and purposeful. You've got to be laser-focused on the prize. The prize is I get my life back and I get my family back. And it's worth whatever valley, whatever mountaintop, to get there.

I was able to experience a little bit of redemption in 2015 when Dan Posthuma produced another multi-artist event called *We Will Stand* and invited me back to sing with The Imperials, like we had tried to do eight years earlier. We sang "Praise the Lord," and it was a beautiful, emotional experience. I'm forever grateful to Dan for this "do-over."

Mark Lowry, comedian

Russ is a legend who just happens to be an alcoholic. I'm not surprised when I find out humans are humans. Just because you're a believer, it doesn't mean you're perfect yet, and it doesn't mean you're not broken. That's why you become a believer—because you are broken, and you need help. In Russ, I've seen a consistent heart that chases after Jesus. And I've seen a consistent love for his family, his children, and all who are in his life.

He and I have talked a lot about grace through the years because we had both been raised with the same kind of spirit—the spirit of legalism. My life changed when I was read *The Grace Awakening* by Chuck Swindoll. In this book, I found out God liked me. He didn't just love me, he liked me. There's a big difference. It's like everything I'd ever hoped about God I found out was true. I found out God really is gracious, that Jesus loved the outcast and the broken. And that it's okay to be broken. Broken pots spill more water, that's what I've always said.

Once your mind has been expanded by grace, you can never get it back into the box of legalism. But all those who are still in the box, say to us, "You're going to go to hell if you live like that." They're wrong. And they end up spending their whole lives walking across a lake that's frozen solid all the way to the bottom. But they're afraid any second that they're going to fall through. Dance on the lake, I say. The way I have forgiven my own mother for not wanting to jump into the discovery of grace with me is that she was walking in all the light she had.

I've seen grace transform Russ by him working it out, going to therapy, and releasing that horrible shame. There's no need for shame. Conviction is a different thing. When I have been in the presence of the Lord and he's convicted me, I've never felt ashamed in his presence. But I have felt ashamed in the presence of his people. Have you seen that bumper sticker that says "Jesus, please save me from your followers?"

Jesus is not the problem. Jesus is gracious.

NINE

DIVING INTO TRAUMA

TORI

Within twenty-four hours of walking out on stage drunk, Russ checked into Cumberland Heights. I was once again left to clean up the mess he had made, and this one was beyond the pale.

I was concerned about the emotional fallout Maddie Rose and Charlotte were experiencing and concentrated on trying to appear calm and reassuring. The truth was I didn't have any idea what my next step should be. My big-hearted sister Liz insisted on coming to Nashville to stay with me and help with the girls while Russ was gone. During the family week program, Liz took the girls up to the lake house, and I took the long drive out to Cumberland Heights every day to sit in group therapy with Russ. He was still very broken and guilt-ridden about the *Timeless* concert disaster and seemed unable to shake it.

Sunday was visitor's day, and I took the girls out to have lunch with him. We were joined at our table by Russ' new friend, the lead singer in a Canadian rock band that Maddie Rose immediately recognized and was thoroughly impressed by. She and Charlotte walked the meditation labyrinth on the grounds and played pool with Russ in the game room. It went well. I was anxious about Russ returning home, but we had a plan in place that included an aftercare program, AA meetings, and intensive therapy with Deb Leinart, who came highly recommended by the Cumberland Heights team. With more than a little apprehension, I agreed to let him come home.

RUSS

The terrible night of the *Timeless* event was the final turning point because it forced me to face what was still broken in me. This would be my third time to go to treatment. I had already learned how to stay sober for long stretches of time, but that volcano of hurt from my past was always just below the surface. Once again, I did everything they told me to do—I didn't fight them, I wanted to get well. But it felt like the lid had been permanently ripped off that volcano when Mom died, and when I left rehab, I was still reeling and shaky. Despite all of the promises I made to myself, it wasn't very long before I just gave up and drank again.

TORI

After Russ came back from Cumberland Heights this time I was definitely thinking, *we'll see if it sticks*. But then there was another relapse. And this was a savage one, different than back in the day. This was self-destructive and horrible. It was like self-inflicted violence because of the intensity of the drinking abuse. As much as he hated himself before he went into treatment for the third time, when he came out and relapsed, all hope was gone.

RUSS

I thought so, too. I thought, *I've tried. My daddy never got out of it. And I'm a Taff. Maybe that's just the way we are.*

TORI

At this point, we obviously knew that most of Russ' problems stemmed from his crippling childhood. This was not news, we had spent years dissecting it in therapy sessions. We didn't have to say, "Gosh, I wonder why he's so unhappy?" That's why what came next was so important.

When Russ relapsed, Deb sat us down and said, "Listen, Russ, it makes no sense for you to go back to treatment yet again. You know how to be sober. What you are is a child of trauma, and that trauma has never been specifically addressed." At that point, I was ready to treat him for anything—pregnancy, malaria, whatever. You know? I didn't care. Just do something that would stop this.

I was fed up to the point that I didn't want to hear anything else about that poor, hurt kid from his childhood. Because all I saw was somebody that was hurting me and hurting our children. I was over it. I was definitely not the loving wife in my prayer closet, standing strong in faith that God was going to smite Russ with sobriety and we'd all live happily ever after. From what I could see, the jury was out on whether either one of us was going to survive.

I used to think that as long as there was any love left for Russ that I'd stay and try to work through it all. When he relapsed this time, which was kind of his last shot, I realized that I could love him *and* leave him. That I could still love him but choose not to be there, for the sake of my health, as well as our children's. *I was living with the product of a mother that should have left.* I'm honestly not blaming Russ' mother, Ann—I understand that she was a product of her environment and that her options were severely limited. But if this is what happens when a child grows up in trauma, I was bound and determined that was not going to happen to mine.

CRY FOR MERCY

I can't do this any longer.
I can't go through this again.
I guess this is what it feels like
to finally reach the end.
And so I'm standing
in the ruins;
I'm reaching out to You.
As I'm sifting through these ashes,
All I know to do
Is cry for mercy,
call for grace.
Give me strength to walk through this place.
And let every tear that slips down my face
be a cry for mercy,
a call for grace.

Am I wrestling with Your angels,
or fighting demons of my own?
Either way I'm losing,
and I'm weary to the bone.
But I want to lay this pain down;
I want to finally learn

that You are the one place
that I can always turn,
to cry for mercy,
call for grace.
Give me strength to walk through this place.
And let every tear that slips down my face
be a cry for mercy,
a call for grace.

Eyes pressed closed to shut out the night.
Heart wide open to let in Your light.
With all my faith, with all my might,
I cry for mercy.

(lyrics by Russ & Tori Taff, Marcus Hummon)

RUSS

Deb told us about a place in Santa Fe, a treatment center that primarily dealt with trauma issues. I didn't have the strength left to fight anybody, but the last thing I wanted to do was to go to yet another expensive summer camp for drunks and let a new bunch of strangers poke at my pain with a stick. But Deb said, "I firmly believe that your core problem is untreated trauma and PTSD, and until that is truly dealt with you're going to continue to relapse every time the pain gets to be unbearable. And that's not going to change until you go all the way down into what really happened to you, look at it, re-experience it, and face just how bad it really was." Then she quietly said, "Russ—what do you have left to lose?" That got my attention. I stood up to walk out of the session, but I stopped at the door and turn around and glared at her. "Okay. I'm trusting you, Deb," I said through clenched teeth.

TORI

After Russ dramatically stalked out of the session, I looked over at Deb and said, "He's 'trusting you'? Wow. Good luck with that!" She knew I was pretty cynical at this point. *Yippee, let's ship him off to another treatment center. How about we drain our retirement savings* (which we did) *and pay for Russ to go talk about himself again for thirty days?* That's what it felt like to me.

The arrangements were made. The Life Healing Center staff determined that Russ was in such bad shape emotionally and physically that they did not want him getting on a plane by himself, so Deb suggested that I fly with him to Santa Fe. This wasn't advertised as a Christian facility, but Deb made sure that they would place Russ with a therapist who shared his belief system because as she said, "Faith is at the root of who he is, and if you don't get that, you're not going to get him."

We got on the airplane, not saying much to each other. I was burned out and bone tired, but I wasn't mad at him anymore. I guess I had finally reached that place that Dr. McMillan had told me about all those years ago. I was done. I wasn't angry, I just wanted to make sure he was safely delivered to the professionals, and then I was going to go home and start making plans. I knew that the marriage was over and that I would be leaving. I hadn't forsaken him. I loved him, but I was done.

There were no tears on that plane ride. I didn't have any left. I was thinking I would probably need to move the girls back to Arkansas, so they'd be surrounded by Mom and Dad, Bud and June, and my brothers and sisters. I knew the three of us were going to need all the family support we could get.

When I dropped Russ off at the center, it was like, *good luck, I love you, goodbye.* I drove to a bed and breakfast I'd booked for the night and slept for almost twelve hours straight. At breakfast the next morning, a couple came and sat down and said, "Hello, how are you? Where are you from?" The people that owned the place called me "Mrs. Taff." The friendly couple said, "Taff's an unusual name. You know, my favorite singer in the world is named Taff." And all I could think of was, *Seriously? Now we're going to sit around and talk about my wonderful husband, the famous gospel singer?*

I told them that Russ and I had flown in together, but I had to head back to Nashville later that day. They said, "Oh, where is Russ staying?" At this point, I was so raw that I simply didn't have the energy to cover for him. I said, "Well, he's at Life Healing Center. He's an alcoholic and he can't stay sober. He had a lot of trauma in his childhood, and they're going to try to help him deal with it." This was further proof that I was done. I wasn't going to protect him anymore. I couldn't protect him from himself.

Call it a message from God. Call it whatever you want. But remarkably, that couple had walked the same journey we were walking, had been to Life Healing Center, and were sitting there whole and restored, taking a romantic weekend together.

They said to me, "Yeah, we were exactly where you are. And you know what? We're together. We love each other." The woman leaned in and said to me, "We have five children and I was done, too."

They hugged me and put me on the plane later that morning, and that's when the tears came. I looked up at the sky and said, "Okay, that was smooth. You basically just put another turtle in the road, didn't You?"

RUSS

I got to Life Healing Center and had no idea what I was getting myself into, except that I was apparently supposed to figure out my entire life in thirty days. I was anxious and skeptical, but I also had a tiny sliver of hope that I was hanging onto. Hope that I could find help for my disease, that maybe my life wasn't over. A sliver.

The Center was in the beautiful Sangre de Cristo foothills overlooking Santa Fe. There were only about thirty patients or so with a low therapist-to-patient ratio, so it was very individualized treatment. They paired me with a therapist named Jason, a kind, funny, intuitive man from West Virginia who was raised in a strict fundamentalist Christian home but had also discovered grace along the way. The first day he told me, "Draw a picture of your higher power." I drew a picture of Jesus, standing over me with his hands on my shoulders, my head turned downward. The staff told me that they weren't going to jump into the hardcore therapy right away because they needed to get me stabilized a little better first. "If we take you down deep into it now, we might not get you back," they said. Not exactly encouraging.

It wasn't too long before things started getting pretty intense. One morning Jason said, "Make sure you bring the picture of Jesus with you to the afternoon session, you're going to need him today." That's when they began experientially leading me back to my very first memories. I had been living most of my life trying to forget these things that happened to me, shoving them down because of the pain they would stir up. I even played mind tricks with myself, saying, *oh that didn't really happen*. I would shut down any therapist who tried to go there previously. Now these people were saying, "We're going to take you there and we'll stay in it as long as we need to stay in it."

I saw myself as a toddler and we walked though some of the things that happened then. My first conscious memory was of stealing baby Earl's bottle away from him and Mama slapping me across the mouth, sending the bottle flying across the room and shattering on the cement floor. Then we moved on to age four, five, six—and seven, when I found Daddy drunk at the house. We'd stay on certain memories for a bit longer before moving onto the next one, identifying and putting words to the feelings that were coming to the surface. It was weeks of painstakingly reliving everything I could pull out of my soul—crying every day, just weeping over the sadness of what happened, and processing all the repressed memories that were flooding back. I brought my picture of Jesus with me every day.

It was exhausting, yet I could feel something spiritual was happening. It felt like every time another hurt would come to the surface, the Holy Spirit would sand it and polish it a little bit and make it to where it was actually okay, it didn't hurt anymore. And then another one. The therapy techniques they were using had fancy unfamiliar names like "prolonged exposure therapy" and "cognitive therapy," but I all I knew was that day after day after day I slowly started feeling better. I didn't feel like I was tiptoeing through a minefield anymore.

Besides the intensive personal therapy, there were all kinds of other classes and workshops that gave me insight into how trauma had affected the way I perceived and experienced life. They taught me about mindfulness and how to be still. They showed me tools to help manage the emotional fallout from what had happened to me, and to cope with the lingering emotional pain.

I physically felt like chains were breaking. Chains that had me nailed to the floor where I couldn't even move. But day after day, I would feel a chain just snap. And, all of a sudden, I can move this arm a little bit. And the next day, *bam*, this one would break. And it kept happening every day.

Before I left Santa Fe, I could finally see my parents as damaged people who had unwittingly passed their generational wounds on down to their children. They were simply trying to find a way out of their own pain. And I could forgive them, because I now understood they didn't purposefully do this to hurt me. I didn't need to continue to rage at what they did to me and my brothers. They didn't have access to the kind of information and help I was getting. They didn't know better.

I even started to recall some happy memories I had buried, which shocked me. It was starting to feel like a miracle had happened, and I wasn't even sure how. But it was real.

One of things that came up during my time at Santa Fe was how my parents never gave me a birthday party—mom and dad were just too busy and stressed out all the time. The message this sent to me was, "You're not worth celebrating."

Some of the therapists decided to throw me a birthday party. They said, "You're eight years old. What do you want for a birthday present?" I surprised myself when without even thinking, I immediately said, "A baseball." I used to love playing baseball, even though I wasn't good at it. I even had a dream once where I was walking through a big rose garden, but instead of roses, it was all the baseballs you could ever want.

The day of the party arrived, and I knew I had to walk into a room where everyone's attention was going to be on me. The introvert side of me kicked into high gear and I began to shake. I told Jason, "I don't know if I can do this. My body is reacting, I don't think I can walk in there." He said, "Just lean on my shoulder and put one foot in front of the other."

Jason basically held me up and walked me into that room. The therapists were smiling and singing "Happy Birthday." There were balloons and a cake. It may sound like a bunch of cliché, touchy-feely therapy stuff, but I was struck with such a powerful outpouring of love and acceptance that it nearly knocked me off my feet, literally. My first reaction was to bat those feelings away with my usual mantra of *I don't deserve it*. But after all of the hard, gut wrenching work I had been doing to lay my demons to rest, I was finally able to receive their love that day. I cried and laughed and cried again.

They honored the eight-year-old in me that day with a birthday party and a beautiful baseball signed by all the therapists and other patients. I keep it in my bookcase, right next to the Grammys.

Michael Tait, Newsboys, dc Talk

Everything about Russ is so real. He's so passionate. For him to have a passionate addiction in the past to alcohol doesn't surprise me. What blesses me is that God delivered him from that. And therein lies the gospel. Sometimes we end up judging people because they sin differently than we do. Instead, let's love them. Let's rehabilitate them with whatever love they need, and not judge them because we're the body. We're supposed to take care of each other.

It's tough when you are a celebrity because people think we don't make mistakes. No, we're just like you. We mess up. There are times I have things in my heart, to be honest, that I can't tell my pastor. Can't tell my best friend, even my sister. There are times you have to go to God and say, "Lord, you have to deal with this sin because it's heavier than I am. It's bigger than I am and the weight's too heavy." I can imagine Russ in those moments thinking, *man, what do I do?* I have people in my life now, thank God, where I can go, "Hey, this is where I am right now, and this is kind of heavy so we'll just kind of keep this between us and let's pray about this." A prayer circle.

I don't think a person is defined by failures or regrets, but how we finish the race. Russ is going to finish this thing strong for God.

TEN

COMING HOME

After Santa Fe, I knew I was going home to a bloody mess. Tori had no reason to trust me. She didn't think I could stay sober. I hoped she would see something in my eyes that she had never seen before. Or maybe how I was handling myself now that might remind her of the young me that she fell in love with.

TORI

When he came back from Santa Fe, he seemed different, but of course I'd seen that before, and it hadn't lasted. I remember Deb looking at me in a therapy session and saying, "You're done, aren't you?" I said, "Yeah. I think I am." I could look at Russ and think, "I'm glad you went to Santa Fe. I truly hope you find some peace, but I don't know if I'm going to be around to see it." I certainly wasn't thinking, *Hallelujah, he's fixed!* The love wasn't gone, but I was pretty emotionally shut down for a long period of time after he got home. My heart was just beat to crap and I didn't have it in me to wait with bated breath to see what was going to happen next.

I knew if I was going to be a single parent, I needed to be around my family. They have always been a real source of strength to me and the girls. So, I'd been checking into houses in Arkansas. I knew that when and if I left, Russ would probably spiral down pretty quickly, and I didn't want the girls to have a front row seat to that.

I was so tired—bone weary to the marrow of my soul tired. I just couldn't do this anymore. And I couldn't trust any of my gut feelings about what direction I should take anymore. I told my brother Matt, "If you see me staying in this marriage for a reason that's not healthy, for a reason that's not good for me or the girls, I need you to promise me that you will tell me." He did, and I believed him.

After that promise from Matt, I decided to go ahead and stay put for now. My one day at a time was waking up in the morning and saying, "Can I be married to Russ today and not be sick?" I meant "sick" in the sense of being stuck in codependency, thinking that I had to save him. Pushing myself beyond my physical and emotional limits, making sure everybody else was okay and ignoring my own needs. That's the sickness of the person who loves an addict. Russ would walk in the door and my anxiety-radar could tell you exactly what kind of mood he was in, what he was feeling. But if you asked me how I felt, I couldn't tell you. In my 12-Step group we have a joke, "You know you're a codependent when you're drowning and the alcoholic's life flashes in front of your eyes."

Even though I decided I could be there for now, I also decided that if I couldn't forgive him, and if I couldn't move past all that had happened to us, then I would have to leave. I'm not the kind of person who wants to live my life sitting up on my moral high horse looking down at my husband. I did not want to live with somebody I had no respect for. I had no desire to walk around with a guilt sledgehammer that I could use on him at any time—"Oh really? Well, do you remember when you…" He had handed me enough ammunition for a lifetime of recriminations if that was the kind of marriage I wanted. It wasn't.

RUSS

And I knew I couldn't live with constant accusations or cold contempt. If Tori needed to make me pay for my sins, how much could I take and still try to get well?

But every time she could have put me in my place, she didn't do it. She had the power to cut my legs out from under me with two words, making me feel completely unworthy, but she never did. I can't tell you what that meant to me. *Yes, I was wrong. Yes, I did all of it.* But she didn't punish me, she didn't rub my nose in my mistakes.

TORI

It's because I knew who Russ was. I remember the early years, the bonding, the person I fell in love with. During the worst of times, when I was watching him destroy that person. I kept saying, "This is not who you are. This is not who you are." And he would tell me, "Yes, it is. I'm a Taff, that's what Taffs do. They screw up."

When he came home from Santa Fe, I started to see that he wasn't just going to meetings and doing the work to get better so that I wouldn't leave. For the first time, I saw him fighting for *himself.* I saw him doing things I never thought he'd do. For instance, Russ was generally very restless; he'd go sit in one place and wouldn't be happy, so he'd go somewhere else and he'd carry the restlessness with him. But for the first time, I saw Russ sitting out on our deck, having a cup of coffee, listening to music or teaching tapes, and he'd just be still. I'd never seen this. I had seen him catatonic and depressed and unable to lift his head, but now his head was up and he was still. I didn't even know what to call it.

After about three weeks of seeing this new Russ, I said, "That's peace. That's what that is." I didn't recognize it because I had never seen it in him. That's when I knew I could stay. Because I wasn't fighting for him all by myself.

Matthew Timm, Tori's brother

My first marriage that lasted fifteen years also involved a spouse who was struggling with alcohol and amphetamine addiction. And it's not that Tori and I compared notes or tried to outdo each other in terms of pain, but I did have personal experience with my own family also being turned upside down by addiction.

What Tori struggled with was the inability to trust what's truth and what's a falsehood, what's real and what's being made up. Russ struggled with feeling so bad about himself, with so much guilt about what he was doing. He felt worthless. He sensed, "I'm messing it up, I'm no good, and I wish I could behave differently. I wish our family could be better and different, but there's no way to snap my fingers and have a magical cure."

I have great admiration for Russ' courage. He has a family history that was very turbulent, very unpredictable, never knowing when things were going to absolutely explode. He carried some of that into the marriage with Tori, as well. It's almost like you're looking over your shoulder and just waiting for the next thing to go wrong. And that's a tough way to live.

The wonderful part about Russ being on the other side of addiction is that I see him relax in some ways that—for literally thirty years—I've never seen him even come close to. He's not always worried that everything's going to come tumbling down. He's a much more relaxed individual, as is Tori, in their relationship and their family as well. That's the best part for me as a family member who loves them both.

Liz Selby, Tori's Sister

I was really protective of Tori. My heart broke for her to have to walk that path. Nobody likes to see anybody that they love suffer, and she did. I can't even tell you how much I admire her for how she stayed and was beside him all the way. And even in the very worst of it, she loved him so much and she just worked hard. I'm not sure I would've had what it took to stay through it, but she did.

There were different times when I was angry at Russ. There were a few years that I just distanced myself a little bit, though I never quit caring for Russ. I mean, he's a terrific, wonderful guy, but the pain that it was causing Tori was hard to watch. And it increased my protectiveness over their little girls. I was mad at him for a while, for what he was putting his family through. We had some tough years. And to watch our parents experience it and worry for Tori, that was tough too.

But when you love somebody, you just forgive.

RUSS

The first months of this were just sheer, nose to the grindstone work. They say, "one day at a time," so I kept telling myself I can do this for another twenty-four hours. And then another twenty-four hours. Then, all of a sudden, I was at thirty days sober. It's all about learning how to live life on life's terms and learning how to accept what *is*, instead of always wanting everything around you to change. I was taking responsibility for what I'd done and standing before God and everybody saying, "I've been wrong. I let something come into my life that I don't want to be there anymore." It really helped me to go to meetings and be around people who are like me—people who had been right at the edge of the abyss and fought their way back. I go to meetings to remind myself that if I bring alcohol into my life again, all that sickness will come back. And I hear what other people do to stay sober another day, and I'm encouraged that I can do that, too.

TORI

We've learned the extreme importance of addressing the connection between untreated trauma and addiction. That was the piece that was missing, keeping Russ trapped in addiction. If this book is simply about a drunk gospel singer who finally gets sober, that's only mildly interesting. But if we're talking a drunk who can't stay sober and doesn't understand why, continually playing out patterns that destroy his life, and *then* he finds his way out—that's when it gets interesting. Especially when the element of trauma is understood.

We all knew Russ had a crappy childhood, but we never thought it would lead to a form of PTSD. I never heard Russ speak about his parents without pain in his eyes. I knew all the stories by heart and I was sick of them. Santa Fe didn't uncover any new information per se, but what came out was just how bad it really was. And that what Russ had been pushing down to protect himself from was so much worse than I thought. I knew there was violence in his home, but I didn't know it was almost daily—from both parents. Those stories I had grown sick of hearing, ended up having a twisted hidden part he hadn't told, which often included young Russ on the floor in the fetal position and somebody kicking him.

It is different than simply having a difficult upbringing. Trauma is what happens to people who experience situations that they're not psychologically, emotionally, or spiritually capable of integrating into their life. When you're a child, your ability to do that is severely limited. Not to mention you're at the complete mercy of whoever the authorities are around you—your parents.

Trauma is what happened to guys in Vietnam. When they came home, they couldn't function. They had been taken out of the life they knew and dropped down into a situation they had never faced before. They had to live in a state of hypervigilance. Every child of trauma has that same thing. It produces cortisol—the dark side of adrenalin. It's the stress hormone that causes a mother to be able to lift a car off her pinned child. They're living with that running through their veins all the time because they're living in a state of heightened alertness, constantly in fight or flight mode. *You've got to be careful. You've got to keep aware.*

It affects you psychologically and physiologically. Sitting down and talking about it helps, but that alone won't make it just dissipate and go away. You have to go all the way back to the earliest memories, the painful parts that you pushed away your whole life and face them down.

Yes, his dad had been abusive. Yes, his mom didn't protect them enough. We knew all of that. But his parents were also capable of being nice people, kind people. If you were sitting next to them right now, you'd like them. They were not monsters. Their actions weren't done out of malice, they were out of ignorance. God only knows what happened to them in their childhood. But the saddest part is if they had laid awake at night and tried to come up with ways to really damage their children, they probably couldn't have done a better job.

But as an adult, Russ had a choice to make: go through life hating an old lady with lupus and her husband—who had the same disease you have—or try to forgive them and move on. He chose the latter, to the best of his ability, but the damage was already done. The voices of shame refused to leave, in spite of the forgiveness. In the Christian world, we want to pray and then it'll be okay. But trauma had literally rewired his brain, in addition to the strong, father-to-son genetic predisposition to alcoholism and depression. A twisted perfect storm. It makes sense now why he thought alcohol was such a wonder drug—his body and mind were sitting ducks for it.

These days I don't live in fear about Russ' sobriety. To be honest, I don't think about it all that much anymore. I know that he wants to be whole and has fought really hard to get where he is now. And he has tools to help him when he gets triggered by something that reminds him of the painful past. It's like a tuning fork goes off and it sends vibrations all the way down to his soul. But he knows how to deal with that now without going off the rails.

Over time, asking myself the question of whether or not I can stay in the relationship simply became irrelevant. There wasn't a day I woke up and suddenly I knew. Life carried us forward from awkward to tentative, to normal, and then to routine.

I certainly don't want to paint a picture of recovery as some sort of fix all—like God waves a wand and it's like it all never happened. Russ' trauma was his childhood. My trauma was Russ' addiction, not to the extent that he had, but it's not too strong of a word to use. Trauma is a profound change that happens in you—physical, mental, emotional, or spiritual—in response to something horrific over a sustained period of time.

But to anyone who finds yourself in a position similar to mine, and maybe you're wondering what your next move should be, God loves you just as much whether you stay or leave. God's love didn't fail you, you have not been forsaken or forgotten. Sometimes you need to leave. I'm grateful that our story is one where Russ and I are still together. But there's no shame in doing what you have to do to protect yourself and your children.

It isn't just our faith in God—or just therapy and good counseling—that make everything better. It's a combination of finding where the help is and using your faith to walk you through that, continually asking for guidance on what to do and where to go.

One thing I've learned about myself through this process is that I run on hope. That's my fuel. But I don't want false hope. I don't want lies. Hebrews 11:1 says, "Faith is the substance of things hoped for, the evidence of things not seen." I think faith is what hope turns into when it grows up.

If I can't see any glimmer of hope in front of me, it sucks the fight right out of me. Amazingly, God knows that's how I work. So, he didn't part the sea or smite Russ with sobriety, but in seemingly small ways over and over, He would put something or someone in my path, and this small ray of hope would start to flicker inside of me. I wouldn't call it faith because I couldn't say, "I absolutely know he's going to be fine." But those little glimpses of hope got me through until I could believe.

So, what do I still believe?

I still believe in a God that cares about me, cares about Russ, and cares about our children. I still believe that our marriage and family are worth fighting for. I still believe that knowledge is power, and that help is out there, even though it may not look exactly the same for everybody. Finding that help is crucial.

Bill Gaither's dad used to say, "You know, people can change…but not very much." I guess that's true, to an extent. Russ is still Russ. I'm still me. I still talk too much. He doesn't talk enough. We're still basically who we were before all this happened, even though we *have* changed in a few very important ways. I still believe in the importance of connection with each other, with other people, with friends, with the community, with the church, with somebody you can trust. That's why we're writing this book—so you don't feel alone in the middle of whatever it is you're going through.

And you know what? If you happen to be reading this and life has shoved you up against the wall so many times that you aren't even sure you still believe in anything, I'll make a deal with you. If you'll just keep waking up in the morning and asking God to help you keep trying to do the next right thing and keep fighting to find and hang onto a tiny glimmer of hope—then I'll keep believing for both of us until you get your miracle, too.

RUSS

Over time, it became more and more clear that God's hand had been guiding me when I didn't even know it. And that I could trust that it will continue to lead.

In the past, I wasn't able to see God's hand. All I could see was my pain. But I can think about my childhood today and I don't hurt. I can think about my childhood today and I'm not angry. I feel sorrow for my parents because they had no tools and they were doing to me what was done to them, I'm sure.

It took all of that for me to surrender and cry out for help. But this Jesus that I've found, I love him so much. He has done just what he said he would do. 2 Corinthians 5:17 says, "If any man be in Christ, he's a new creation. Old things pass away, and all things become new."

Just a few months after coming home from Santa Fe, my body and mind had reached a place of healing. But God had something more in mind that I didn't see coming. Tori and I were down in Texas visiting Mark Lowry and some friends. While we were there, Mark's pastor called and said that his father, Bishop Jones, was dying of cancer. His dad, who had served the church for forty-four years, loved the DVD that Bill Gaither did on me. Dena, Mark's childhood friend who had grown up in that church, asked me if there was any way I could stop by the hospital as a special surprise for her beloved pastor. I had planned on hitting an afternoon AA meeting anyway, so I figured as long as I was out, I could swing by. I loaded my acoustic guitar in the car, and Peggy Campolo and Dena rode along with me. I thought I would make a brief appearance, sing a couple of songs, and then go back to Mark's and eat Mexican food. My good deed for the day.

When I walked into the hospital room, I stopped dead in my tracks. The man lying in the hospital bed looked so much like my dad, it absolutely floored me. I didn't know whether to turn and run or what to do. He had hair like my dad. He had big hands like my dad. Blue eyes like my dad. I was seriously taken aback, but I took a step and went in.

Pastor Jones saw me, threw his hands in the air and said, "Oh, Russ," and tears started running down his face. The first thing he said to me was, "You know, I taught my boys how to live, and if God doesn't heal me, I'm going to teach my boys how to die." That's the heart of a father.

I took my guitar out of its case and said, "Pastor Jones, what do you want to hear?" And he said, "Heartbreak Ridge," then "O Say, But I'm Glad." His sons Brett and Scott were grinning from ear to ear, filming the whole thing on their phones for the family members that couldn't be there. I sang for about forty-five minutes and I could see he was getting pretty tired.

I packed up my guitar and was about to leave when he said, "Russ, would you mind praying for me?" I couldn't fathom coming up with anything that would do justice to the moment. I just laid my hands on his arms and prayed the best I could. When I finished I looked at him and said, "Pastor Jones, would you pray for me?" I immediately wanted to reach out and pull back those words. I have no idea why I even said that because he was tired and I was ready to leave. But he immediately said, "Oh Russ, I'd love to."

That's when the miracle began. Pastor Jones asked his sons to help him get up out of bed, then he stood on the floor next to me, and put his hands on my shoulders. I'm looking up at him like I used to with my own dad. He began to pray, and I began to cry. I collapsed to my knees and cried harder and harder, sobbing like a child—fifty years' worth of bottled up tears. He pulled my head to his belly, stroked my hair, and began to affirm me like a father. He said, "Russ, Jesus is so proud of you and what you've done with your life. He loves how you've used your talent for his kingdom." The more this pastor, this father who looked like mine affirmed me, the deeper I cried. "Continue to guide him, Father. Let him feel the embrace of the body of Christ." I don't know how long he held me, just stroking my hair and speaking those words of life over me.

Something happened in that moment on a spiritual level that I've never experienced before or since. Things began to shift in me, I could physically feel it happening. God's love was pouring over me like a balm, a blessing, a benediction. And I let it in.

When I returned to Mark's house, Tori took one look at me and said, "What happened to you?" It was that obvious from thirty feet away. I just shook my head and said, "I can't talk about it yet." I had no words to express how the Holy Spirit had just reached down into the bottom of my soul and gathered up the last broken pieces of my childhood. And that God loved me enough to orchestrate the whole thing just for me. I thought I was going to go sing for a guy. But my Father had spent years preparing the way, getting me ready for the moment He would bring in a father who could affirm me in a way my own Dad never could. And I was free.

That day, I stepped out of the role of a traumatized child trying to get well. In that moment, I became a man. Now I would be able to turn and affirm my children and the people around me because that wounded child wasn't looking for daddy anymore. Everything changed and fell in order—my mind, body, and spirit all connected that day.

Chonda Pierce, Comedian

Tori had been very honest with me about Russ' struggle with addiction because I had been very open and vocal about my husband's struggle with alcohol. What I needed at that particular time was understanding, because I didn't understand what was going on in my life. There was no one in the limelight that I knew who was willing to talk about what was really going on in their lives or the struggles that they had.

I'll never forget Tori calling me up and inviting me for dinner. That quick little dinner wound up being four and a half hours of me sitting there asking, "What do I do?" She and I talked about the fear of this news of my husband being a terrible addict coming out because then people would say, "Well, you shouldn't have been on the road. You should have been home more." At some point, especially in the Christian world, you would think we could be a little more merciful and grace-giving. It was great to talk to someone who was walking this journey out.

I didn't want to be a co-conspirator in keeping secrets but living in the limelight and having a husband that's an alcoholic can force you to do that. I knew Tori has had to be a co-conspirator, so here was a chance for two women to look at each other and go, "Okay, when is the right time to blow the whistle? When is the right time to speak up? And how do you navigate that?" Hiding is another tool Satan tries to use to destroy you. We were coming out of hiding together.

The best advice she gave me was what *not* to take ownership of. I can do all that I can do to be a supportive wife, but if David was going to drink, David was going to drink, and there was nothing I could do. I can pour it all out and refuse to have it in my house. I can set boundaries and say, "If you drink again, this is going to happen," and I can follow through with all of that. But I cannot make him stop drinking. That's what I needed to hear from Tori.

As the wife of an alcoholic, you struggle with how much of it is your fault. I would work to have a meal on the table when he walks in from work, hoping he'd say, "What a babe I married." But when he would come in, staggering from stopping to drink after work, I couldn't help but wonder, "What am I doing wrong here?" The wife of an alcoholic takes on that feeling of, *there's got to be something I can do. There's got to be a way I can change him.* Or, *what am I doing wrong? Am I contributing to this? And does he not love me enough to want to stay sober?*

Talking to Tori was the first time I looked across the table and another wife was going, "Yeah. Yeah. I know exactly what you're talking about. Been there. Got the t-shirt, girl." I would say something, and she'd go, "Oh, no, no. Stop. Stop. Now that's wrong thinking right there. No, you can't go there." Because she'd been down that road.

Any one of us probably have a pile of dysfunction or pain or something difficult that could break that bond that you have with God at any moment. People have had lesser things that made them walk away from their faith. But witnessing a story like Russ and Tori's gives people like me the courage to fight through our stuff and hang on.

THIS LOVE IS STRONG

Sometimes the questions
Seem so hard
Are we growing together
Or falling apart
The ghosts of the past
Have infected our dreams
What's the damage, what's the cost
Are we destined to repeat
I remember at the start of it
Our hopes were still new
Our eyes were wide with innocence
Our hearts were strong and true
We trembled as we fought to keep our

First love alive
When did things get out of hand
How do we survive

This love is strong, it will last
It will hold you up when you need it
It will not break, I won't give up
It costs too much and I need you

We circle like opponents
Sparring with the blame
You hold your heart so tightly
To shield it from more pain
But even now sometimes I see
Unguarded in your eyes
That fragile hope that love can win
The willingness to try
It's such a complicated thing, it's not easy
I'm here for you, when you need me
We'll fight to hold the ground we've won, please don't surrender
We're not in this alone

(lyrics by Russ & Tori Taff)

Joseph Habedank, Southern Gospel Singer

Russ is probably one of the kindest human beings I've ever met. And his character, even with all his flaws that he's so open about, is just unmatched. I met him shortly after I lost my job singing with a very successful Southern Gospel group called The Perrys. I was their lead singer/songwriter for ten years and got hooked on pain pills. They gave me numerous chances and I just couldn't get clean—I needed help. They graciously allowed me to resign. A couple days later I checked into Cumberland Heights for a thirty-day stay.

About a week into my treatment, one of the counselors came to me and said, "There's somebody here that wants to have lunch with you." I walked into the dining room, and there sits Russ Taff—who I recognized, of course, and was immediately intimidated. Little did I know, Russ has no judgment whatsoever and made me feel so at home.

We talked about what I had been through as a child from a broken home. And he could see, I think, so much of himself in me. He looked at me and said, "You know, Joseph, Jesus loved you when you were using drugs. But he's crazy about you now." That changed everything for me—as rotten, filthy, and wretched as I felt, to be told that Jesus didn't just love me, but he was crazy about me.

I asked him that day if he'd be willing to be my sponsor and he said, "Absolutely, I'd be honored." Every day I would call him he made me feel like, not only could I beat this, but that I wasn't a bad person. Jesus still loved me. People would still accept me. But I'd have to be honest with myself and with him.

In the beginning of my recovery, I was thinking, *how in the world am I going to stay sober for a year?* Russ was always very focused on the present moment. He'd say, "Let's worry about what's going on right now. Can you stay sober tonight?" I said, "Yeah, I think I can stay sober tonight." Then he'd say, "Okay, cool. Let's get through tonight. And then tomorrow we'll talk about tomorrow." It was such a big thing for me to realize all I have is right now. And if I can stay sober today, if I can stay clean today, that's great. We'll worry about tomorrow when it gets here.

I'll never forget how much emphasis Russ put on my relationship with my wife Lindsay. What a lot of people don't realize is that while addicts get help, their families don't. Addicts can go to treatment, but their families can't, so they're stuck trying to recover on their own from this awful disease of addiction. A big thing for me was learning how to not only recover, but how to be a recovering husband and be good to my wife.

Let's face it. If you're an addict or an alcoholic in the secular world, you go to rehab and your stock kind of goes up—you get press. As they say in Hollywood, and even in Nashville, any press is good press. In the gospel world, it's a little different. You go to rehab and it's more like, *I don't know if this guy can come back*. There are people who haven't been able to bounce back. But what's crazy to me is that we often forget the focus of our music is redemption, forgiveness, mercy, and grace. When somebody falls, especially one of our own, we ought to welcome them back and love them.

Russ gave me hope that I could have a career in gospel music again. He'd say, "It may not feel like it right now, but you're going to sing again. And it's going to be better, better than it's ever been. Because now you have a story to share. They'll be able to tell the realness of what God's done in your life." That was the biggest thing that helped me to realize that I could sing again. I could do this because he did it. He was the ultimate inspiration for me.

Russ made me believe that Jesus loved me, no matter what. He showed me what it means to be a man—a real man who falls, gets up, dusts himself off, does the next right thing, and recovers every single day. Not only is Russ one of my heroes and my friend, but he saved my life.

FARTHER ON

I hear you have a soft spot
For fools and little children
And I'm glad
'Cause I've been both of those
I shook my fist up toward the sky
And at most of those who love me
A frightened angry boy
In grown-up clothes

But a father's eye
Can always see right through
And a father's heart
Can tell when tears are true
Now I'm standing on this road
Your hand has brought me to
Your faithful love will lead me
Farther on

Life sure has its choices
You left those choices to me
And I'm glad
But sometimes I feel caught
It's hard to know which bridge to cross
And which bridge I should be burning
I long to learn
But I'm so slow at being taught

(lyrics by Russ & Tori Taff)

ELEVEN

WHAT HOPE LOOKS LIKE

TORI

What's interesting about this process of writing a book is that it does kind of make you relive the bad stuff. But it's not a knife in the heart anymore. Now when we talk about the past, I don't see guilt in Russ' face. We can revisit those places, feel a twinge of pain, and move on. That's what healing looks like to me. I don't remember a specific moment where a big wave of *now we're fine* hit me and then the angels sang. It's just that we don't live there anymore.

Back when we first got married, I thought our life was going to be a series of wonderful adventures, experiencing everything side by side with my buddy Russ. When all that started falling apart, we both began to see each other as the flawed human beings we are, the sum total of everything we've gone through, for good and for bad. Even without addiction, life kind of does that to you in a long-term marriage, anyway. Reality sets in.

Anybody who's married to an alcoholic has a love/hate relationship with hope. You don't really want to indulge in it very much because every time you do, you get let down. Sometimes spectacularly, sometimes in small ways. But even now, the carrot on the stick that keeps me moving forward every day is hope—it's just the way I'm wired. I love the feeling that life is full of possibilities and there might be something amazing right around the corner. Addiction almost kicked that out of me, but thank God, it didn't.

A different kind of hope was being birthed in recovery. It wasn't the kind where you cross your fingers and hope that Russ comes home sober or doesn't do something to blow our lives up again. Hope began to creep in when I realized that I wasn't asking myself, "Can I be married to him, today and not be sick?" I don't exactly know when it stopped, but there was a point when it became a moot point—I was in it. Hope changed into something more resembling a grounding, a foundation, that felt pretty solid. Something we could build on.

This is also how forgiveness came. I didn't make a magnanimous gesture and my heart was right and I was able to suddenly forgive Russ for everything—I wish it had happened that way. I told God, "I'm not going to force anything here. It would be a joke if I did. You know me better than anybody. I'm not a grudge-holder, but I don't *feel* forgiveness. I feel wariness." So, I prayed, "I'm willing to forgive. But You're going to have to do the heavy lifting." I was not so wrapped up in my own sense of "I was wronged" that I wanted to hang on to that.

It's easy to be the healthy one by default when you're in a relationship with someone who's addicted because the bar is set pretty low. It's really easy to just say, "God, fix him and bring him back when You're done." But addiction is a family disease and everybody gets affected. I realized that I also had a lot of work to do because I could see I was stuck in patterns that weren't healthy. So, it wasn't just Russ that had to change. This was a journey that both of us had to roll up our sleeves and get serious about.

Trust goes both ways. I didn't betray his trust in the same ways that he betrayed mine. I wasn't acting out, I wasn't an alcoholic, but Russ didn't trust people easily at all. He was always waiting for the other shoe to drop. He learned, literally at his father's knee, that the hand that reaches out, that you think is going to stroke your head, can slap your face. And you never know which one it's going to be.

While my trust went away in increments, it also came back in increments. Don't get me wrong—triggers can still happen, and all of a sudden, I'm slammed back into defense mode. But I learned to not live constantly with my dukes up because for so long it felt like I had to protect myself and the girls from the uncertainty of what Russ might do next. Being able to gently, in small ways, begin to lay that down and lean in again, was huge. But it took a while.

I also had to realize that part of our healing together was not just me being able to trust him again—that he's not going to go out and get drunk. It was Russ being able to trust me enough to be vulnerable with me. And to know that I loved him no matter what. That he's not on probation. I knew that for many years, every time he looked at me I was simply one more reminder of how bad he was screwing up. That's not a fun role to have, it's certainly not one I asked for. It turned me into a cartoon character in his mind—the screeching wife chasing him around the kitchen with a rolling pin. He had to learn to trust that it was safe to lean in to me, too.

The emotional intimacy between us and the physical intimacy between our bodies were both hit equally hard. I didn't want to have sex with an angry, defiant teenager or an emotionally crippled child. And for a long, long time it felt like that's who I was living with. I wanted a partner, another grown-up in the house. But instead, I had this needy, self-centered, depressed kid, or this sullen adolescent who was doing the emotional equivalent of peeling out and slinging gravel around to make a point. There wasn't anything sexy about either scenario.

Intimacy is all wrapped up in trust. I was raised by a mother who didn't shame us about anything that had to do with human sexuality and so, I didn't have a lot of baggage in that area. That was always a part of our marriage that was fun and healthy. But it did take a hit when I didn't trust him—I did not want to open myself up to him on any level.

When we started getting back into the day-to-day routine after Santa Fe, and were picking kids up, getting groceries, and he was going out on the road and coming back, I started feeling like I had a friend. We weren't partners yet, but I had a friend in the house. I didn't keep him too close, but I enjoyed being with him.

One day, I had something I needed to talk about regarding the kids. I was used to calling my brother, Matt, the child psychologist—which is handy—or calling a girlfriend. But Russ was there, and I started talking to him. This was very new at this point. But Russ physically leaned in while we were talking. All of a sudden, I realized that I'm risking my feelings and being really vulnerable with him. And it felt right. I don't think I'd use the word "safe" at this point, but that's where we were headed.

I gradually started enjoying him again—his sense of humor, the way he was with the girls, even singing. I originally fell in love with the man, not the voice, and he never listens to his music at home. But he'd be on stage and I'd think, "Look at that. He's really amazing." And gradually, in tiny increments, I started enjoying him. That was the biggest hurdle. It wasn't about starting to love him again, I always loved him. I knew I couldn't force my heart to feel forgiveness. But when I started enjoying him again, then I knew God was working out the forgiveness part in me, and that trust was returning. We hadn't had fun together in a long time at that point, so to just feel simple, uncomplicated pleasure in being around him was a really big deal.

The most attractive he has ever been to me is when I am dealing with a grown-up in his adult space—that's truly all I have ever wanted. When he's in the child space, that's where the shame is. And where the shame is, that's where the pain is—the blaming and the need to hide.

RUSS

I always knew the easier option would be to divorce her and not have to deal with all this anymore. Just start off fresh somewhere else. Although, the truth is that I would've simply taken all of my pain and everything else to another relationship. But when I committed to the hard work of getting well, and learning to love again, I prayed, "Jesus, I'm committing to this path. Now would you help me?"

I'd been away from her in Santa Fe for sixty-five days. I was nervous coming home, mostly because I didn't know what she was thinking. Was she checked out already? Or was she willing to do the hard work with me? When I got home and saw that she was willing to stay and fight for us, and I knew I was willing to stay and fight, that's when I knew we had a chance. I knew with God's help, I was going to work to win her back. And if I could, I'd know it's Him.

At first, I felt her not pulling away from me, per se, but also not embracing me. It's like we would both stick out a finger and gradually they'd touch. And pretty soon you hold out your hand, and she gradually holds out her hand, perhaps during a time when she realizes I'm really listening to her, hearing her concerns.

But when I saw that things between us was starting to get better, I would just gently ask her a work-related question. "What do you think should be done about this?" And she would think about it a little bit, and then say, "This is what I think, but it's just my opinion." The more I kept doing that, the more she'd respond. She could see that I trusted her brain. That's when I saw we were making progress because she was starting to get interested in my work again.

Things that used to be so natural and normal early on were all new again. We had to figure out how to do it—something even as simple as walking through the mall. When you've gone through such a traumatic experience together, it takes a while before you can hold her hand and mean it. And she holds your hand and means it as well.

It was a big deal just to hold her hand. And then she would let me kiss her some. It wasn't as if, as soon as you get home, all this wonderful stuff happens. It takes a while to take all that information, all that healing, and bring it back to where it can go deep inside both of us and I can be the man I truly want to be. Even when we couldn't communicate, there were times we would make love and I would feel a glimpse of connection we had in the past and it gave me hope.

What held us so much is our faith in Jesus and trying to follow His voice and direction. And not listening to outside voices that would encourage us to run away from each other. Voices that said, "How can you live with that?" I even had guys saying, "Man, I'd hate to be married to your wife."

Tori: *Wait. What?*

Russ: *They say, "She's got a thousand questions and she just comes at you like the inquisition." And I would say, "Yeah. if you want to view it that way, she does."*

Tori: *Ok, I'll give them that one. But only because I'm such a delightful ray of sunshine in every other way.*

When Tori would come at me with a lot of questions, I would stand there and take it and not get offended. I wouldn't say, "How dare you say something like this to me." Because I knew she was right. It took her awhile to settle down and put her dukes down to where she wasn't watching me out of the corner of her eye all the time. She came back genuinely to try and make it work. She could've threatened me, but she didn't.

I wanted her to see who I was turning into, and that she and I could experience some joy again after it had all been so hard and dark. The thing that held us together when we were younger was our sense of humor. We could laugh at anything. But when the trouble hit, all that went away.

I couldn't help but wonder, "Will Tori be able to let go of all my mistakes from the past?" I told so many lies to cover up my drinking. I would come home smelling like beer and she'd say, "How many have you had?" And I'd say, "Oh, just a couple." When the truth is, I had eight. I wasn't being honest at all.

I knew there were times she thought I was the biggest hypocrite in the world—standing on those stages, saying one thing and then going back to my room and doing another. I don't blame her. It troubled me just as much that I was doing exactly what my dad did—where he would stand and preach on Sunday, and then three months later he'd be passed out drunk in a bed.

I knew I had changed and was *still* changing. I couldn't help but wonder, "Who am I going to be when this healing is complete?" It's a valid question because I was changing so much. I was liking what was happening with me, but would Tori like it? Maybe I could be the person she wants or needs. Maybe I could be the kind of husband she could respect.

With the black cloud of addiction no longer hovering over our heads, we finally had the freedom to discover who we are and what we want. We didn't have to live every minute wondering if we were going to stay together or what was going to happen next.

The big thing that was different after Santa Fe was that my thoughts were about Tori more than they were about me. "What can I do to help her be happy again? What can I do to get out of the way and let her become the person God created her to be?"

Through our whole marriage, I never tried to critique her or contain her. I'm not the kind of person that's going to say, "You need to wear that dress," or "You need to do this." I know some men are like that, but I just wanted her to be who she is. I never wanted to get in the way and mess it up. More than ever, I wanted her to find her way—for her to be happy again, to enjoy life like she used to.

Addiction had made me such a self-centered person. It was all about me getting what I needed whenever I needed it, no matter how it affected anybody else, which is so contrary to my true nature. But that was subdued by my drinking. It makes sense that I was so miserable trying to live in a way that is contrary to my true self. I could see the way I wanted to be, but I felt powerless to get there.

What's amazing is what happens when you allow Jesus to take over. That is what I had to do. I had to lay all my burdens and cares on Him and trust Him to do great work. I knew that God desired for us to stay together. I know some people can't. But for us, we had that spark in our marriage that kept saying, "I think we can do it." Over and over. And then very slowly, the roots began to come together again. Our fear was being covered by God's love.

In Santa Fe, I learned how to be an adult and not just a wounded kid that's constantly yelling, "Hey everybody, look at my pain!" They had done so much difficult work digging into my past, the pain, the trauma, and together we pulled up the weeds. Even in my relationship with Jesus, I was maturing and turning into an adult.

For so many years, I didn't trust myself to carry the weight of being a responsible husband for her. But I was beginning to believe I could.

Maddie Rose Taff, daughter

At Life Healing Center, dad was given tools and things to deal with the demons and the scars that he had. Even though this was one of the worst things that has happened to us, at the same time, I have a dad now that I never would have had otherwise. I mean, I'm not going to necessarily say that I'm grateful for it because it was really painful, but if this is what it took to get him to where he's at now, I'm grateful. He's present. He's loving. He's engaged. He's one of the wisest people I know. I'm grateful for that place. If there's anything I can say about my dad, it's that he's a fighter.

My advice to anybody going through something similar would be to find your Higher Power and hold them hard. If it wasn't for the God of my understanding, I couldn't have gotten through this. I needed that hope. I needed to feel held when I wasn't being held.

When he came back from Santa Fe, there was still chaos, but it was a different kind of chaos—mostly from trying to integrate dad back into the family. Sometimes at night I would climb out the window and get up on top of the roof of our house and look up at the stars and the moon. That's when I would talk to God and that's when I felt held. Those were the times that I knew I was looking up and somebody was looking back, and that somehow, in some way, things were going to be okay. I was going to understand normal again. I was going to understand life again. That's my advice to anybody going through this— find your Higher Power and hold on tight.

I have a friend and a dad now. He's a goofball. I can trust him again and feel like I can go to him for anything now. He understands and he's present. I just love that guy.

TORI

I'm so respectful of the work Russ has done—and respect is a big deal. It's one of the hardest things to get back after it's lost. My respect for Russ is not because he's returned to being the same guy I fell in love with—he couldn't possibly be that guy forty-some years later. But this is the grown-up version of Russ that was always in there—the man who has a heart for God, who I can lean into and trust, and look up to.

Reclaiming trust in our marriage didn't look like hearts and flowers. It wasn't presents, poems, and sentimental cards. What it looked like was ditch-digging, dirt under the fingernails, jack-hammering hard work, done by two people seeking to understand each other and themselves, in order to remake a marriage. It doesn't sound very romantic, but when you see somebody put in what it takes every day, whether he feels like it or not, that's when you begin to trust. Because someone can say all the right words to you but seeing them put in the work makes all the difference. I was watching Russ do what it takes. And that's truly the most romantic part to me. Because it worked.

After Santa Fe, we had something to go back to—a frame of reference. We built a strong foundation of love and friendship over the first ten years of marriage—we traveled all over the world, we connected with each other. Even though that got blown to smithereens with addiction, no one could take away those great times together. Addiction takes a sledgehammer to everything good in your life. But for us, underneath the rubble, there was still something healthy. We might have been young and stupid back then, but our connection was real.

Part of what keeps us liking each other is that at this point, we're kind of foxhole buddies. We're the only ones who can look at each other, and say, "Gosh. Remember that? Remember how horrible it was?" And by the same token, we're the only ones who share the exquisitely good memories, like exploring the world together, writing songs, watching our girls being born. Sifting through our past and writing about it does bring up some hard, hurtful times. But I don't feel blame. I just feel grateful. I love Russ. That kind, funny man with a huge heart was always in there. He just had a lot of stuff in there covering it up.

Neither Russ nor I ever wanted a fake Christian marriage where people pat me on the back and say, "Oh, you're such a saint to have stayed." Let me just make it clear that Russ wasn't the only angry one around the house. I was not sitting in a corner sweetly interceding for him. I wanted to kill him dead. I hated what I saw, and I hated who he was becoming. I was furious, I felt like I got gypped. This isn't the guy I married. What the heck! I didn't even waste my anger on God, it was all aimed at Russ.

There was a lot of anger to go around. Obviously, there was a lot that needed to be unraveled and looked at in me as well. Addiction is a family disease. The addict's behavior doesn't happen in a vacuum. And likewise, they don't heal in a vacuum.

We are still living everyday with the sum total of everything that's ever happened to us, good and bad. These days, we've got a lot more good. Though there was a time when it looked like the bad was overwhelming us, to the point where there were days I couldn't even remember the good things between us. It was simply the present struggles demanding all my focus. But, all these years later, we now have a shared history. Pain is bonding if you survive it.

And just in case you were wondering (I wouldn't blame you!), Russ wasn't drunk or drinking the vast majority of the time he was out performing concerts over these past forty years. Those episodes were mercifully rare, relatively short-lived and inevitably ended up with him going to treatment. He had extended periods of sobriety, up to ten years at a time. And when he did relapse, almost all of his drinking was done when he was back in Nashville. Russ completely owns and takes responsibility for every mistake and bad decision he ever made during his battle with alcoholism. The miracle is that God showed up in spite of Russ' brokenness and somehow used his music to reach people all over around the world.

Bill Gaither

I know of no one in the Christian music field who is loved as much as Russ is loved. I first saw him perform with The Imperials at the Christian Booksellers Association back in the early '80s. I had never met him, but I thought, "This is quite a charismatic young character." When we finally connected one to one, it was great. He told me he used to come to the Barton Coliseum in Little Rock and see the Bill Gaither Trio as a kid. He said he had a crush on Gloria, and that he remembered her doing those "readings" that she did. It was just very moving to him. We started talking, and building our relationship through our artist retreats, Homecoming events, our time together in the Vocal Band, and even taking trips together with Russ and Tori.

I learned that Russ and I both grew up in experiential churches. His happened to be Pentecostal, mine was Holiness. The thing they both had in common was an open altar, where young and old would come forward and pray during the public services Sunday morning or Sunday night, or once a night, in our case. Some people would say while they're praying that they're coming to get saved, others would say they're coming to be sanctified.

Later on, we finally were able to admit that even after we were saved and sanctified that we still needed help. It is very tough for a kid growing up in an experiential church to say exactly when he got saved. For that kid, every trip to an altar wasn't about getting saved again, he was thinking in terms of, "I slipped and did not know the words to put on that." When you talk in terms of salvation with Russ, I think you have to say it is a daily, daily, daily thing.

The thing that I admire about Russ the most is that he just doesn't give up. There's always another level that he is honest enough to say, "I'm not there and I need to do something about it." I don't know of anybody humbler and farther away from the word pride than Russ. I also know that one of Russ' greatest gifts is that he's still able to laugh at himself. I think we need to take God very seriously and not take ourselves very seriously.

I would hope that through all of this, the wisdom Russ has gained from all of this could be used to help others. I wish for him some wonderful days of ministry where churches would have him in to tell his story. In the past they probably said, "Why don't you sing more and talk less?" to where now they'll say, "Why don't you sing less and talk more?" These could be really great days for him.

RUSS

It's a bit like salvation. You receive Jesus as your Savior—that's the easy part. Then He starts working to change your character. He starts working to make you honest. And it's work. After you receive Christ, that's when the work really begins, to where you have His nature and your nature butting heads until you finally learn to just submit to Him. And then after a while, you begin to trust Him.

I kept saying, "If I just love her unconditionally, God can do the rest." It was all about me doing the hard work I had to do and then trusting God for the miracle.

I always knew in my gut that when the time was right to tell my story, I would know. So here we are. I'm coming out of hiding. I'm declaring that I'd rather be an honest person, living authentically, showing you my wounds and scars, than constantly trying to hold up a persona of someone who has it all together. I want to live free, declaring the power of hope, grace, and relentless love.

I've experienced the never-ending, ever-pursuing love of God. I've also seen this fierce love demonstrated from Tori, who to me, is the true champion of this story. She fought for me when I couldn't fight for myself. I've experienced relentless love from Bud and Mama June and my Smedley family. Tori's family never turned against me, they loved me and always held out hope that I would get well. I've been surrounded by the love of people in the music industry who not only appreciated what I did, but they also protected me and prayed for me. I have been treated with loving care by all the therapists and counselors whose paths I have crossed. I can also now see that my Mama and Daddy loved me—it was an imperfect love, yes. But they were two hurting, damaged people who never had the luxury of getting the kind of help that Tori and I did. They were doing all they knew to raise me how they thought was best.

Nobody but God is able to love us perfectly. I wish I was able to love Tori and my daughters perfectly. I'm doing better than I used to, that's for certain. I wish my parents had been able to love me better. I wish I would've been able to love myself better. But to love, and be loved, means a certain amount of grace and mercy have to be continually extended back and forth—in great abundance. And somehow in the middle of our imperfect attempts at love, and our choosing to keep extending grace, God shows up and loves us in ways others can't.

My prayer for you is that you're able to let yourself be loved by God, but to also grow in how you can love and forgive other people. Many of us are walking around carrying some pretty big wounds, keeping our true selves under wraps, so no one knows. Find some people who you can be completely honest with and listen to their stories. Hear God whisper in your ear that you're loved, and that your wounds and defects don't define you.

And then find someone you can help. Someone you can encourage. Let them know they are not alone and pour hope on them that life can be better, that relationships can be better, that God's love is real.

Our struggles try to keep our focus on ourselves, so we aren't able to see or feel God and the needs of people around us. They tempt us by saying, "No one will ever understand. No one has it as bad as you." These are lies. You are not writing the book on pain and misery. And actually, you're a lot less unique than you thought.

Something I heard in a meeting once is, "Welcome to the *normal* section." Many of us have thought we were living in the "special" section our whole lives. Whether it was the section for people who have been hurt worse than everyone else or people who are simply superior to others. When we open our eyes to others and hear their stories, we find out that we all have a lot more in common than we could have ever imagined. This is when hope shows up.

I'm telling my story, so God can get the glory for all that he has done for me and my family. I'm grateful to be living in a place of confidence now that I believe I can make it through another day. The odds are in my favor that I'm not going to fall back into the old behavior. I'm leaning on God so strongly.

I can be grateful now for the pains, the struggles, the scars, and the hurts because I have found something that is so real. I feel blessed that I have been able to walk through all of this rubble, learning and growing each day. I'm starting to feel like an adult in the kingdom of God where most of my life I was simply a young child with battle scars. I've walked through situations that should have destroyed me, but I didn't quit.

I'm not perfect. There are still so many things the Holy Spirit is working with me on. There is a saying from AA that is my current mantra: "I'm not where I want to be, but thank God, I'm not where I was." Every year, every week, every day, I can look back and see progress. That keeps me going.

TORI

Russ and I talk a lot about therapy, treatment, and programs but those are not just buzzwords to us. They are life-saving tools. When you're dealing with addiction, abuse, and trauma, taking full advantage of all of the help and knowledge available out there is crucial. You cannot fix what you don't know is broken. You cannot fight an enemy that doesn't have a name. And you can't change deeply ingrained patterns if you don't learn how to recognize them. Therapy is not a substitution for faith in God—in our case, it was quite literally the visible hand of God. Every stumbling step that we took towards wholeness was mercifully and gracefully guided by our Higher Power. He brought us who we needed, exactly when we needed them. There was *this* person who was there when Russ was first diagnosed with addiction, then *this* person who started dealing with our relationship issues, then *this* person who led us to the trauma work. We certainly don't assume that our way is the only way. We can only speak of our own experience and tell you what our process looked like.

And one more thing—don't ever let lack of finances keep you from seeking help. Twelve Step meetings are free and *everywhere* all over the world. Celebrate Recovery is in 35,000 churches nationwide. There are counseling centers in every state that offer sliding scale fees based on income. There is help available out there, but you have to take responsibility for your own recovery. Just reach out and take the first step— God will meet you there.

RUSS

I spent most of my life trying to follow a God that did not like me—a God who was cruel and hard. It took me crashing several times before I would let go of that false God and start looking at who Jesus is. I had thought I was abandoned. I thought I was all alone. But as I began to look back, I saw Him everywhere. I saw that he was with me when I was seven years old and Daddy got drunk. My parents would never come to my Little League games, but I could see Him in the bleachers, cheering. And when I did my first concert with the Sounds of Joy and I played a guitar solo, in my mind I saw Him giving me a wave in the crowd. And He was proud of me. I felt His pleasure, like I was doing something right. He was there that first time I got drunk and my heart was broken. He was there.

But when I realized that He would go down into the mud and dirt to get me, that I'm His kid and He doesn't walk away from His kids, that's when I began to lift my head up a little bit.

Grace says, "There's nothing you can do to earn God's love, it's given to you as a free gift. You no longer have to work so hard to try to gain my approval, my love, my respect. It's already yours because you are my child. I love you and I enjoy you. You are forgiven for all the things you've broken, all the things you have damaged, all the times you tried to disappear. I have always been with you, loving you, holding you, caring for you. All those times you felt you needed to hide, I was right there with you. You are mine."

TORI

I have a lot of hope these days. I hope that we live and die in this quirky little town that we love, surrounded by all these weird, artsy people that we have found community with. I live with the hope that we're going to watch our girls find the right partners in their lives and blossom, and maybe we'll have grandchildren, though as our friend Mark Lowry tells us, we'll probably be in diapers ourselves by that time since we were such late bloomers.

Interestingly enough, none of my hopes for the future are dependent on whether Russ drinks again or stays sober. Perhaps part of my healing is that my life is not all wrapped up in making sure Russ stays okay. I truly pray that he does. I trust his desire to live in recovery. I'm a person who is choosing another person to live out our lives together. And I'm very happy with that decision.

We belong together.

Russ: *And that's Tori getting the last word.*
Tori: *Of course, just how God intended the book to end.*
Russ: *You're right.*
Tori: *You're welcome.*

EPILOGUE

TO TORI

When I hated myself, you loved me for some reason. And when I tried to get away from myself, you saw something in there. When I was denying it, you reminded me that my true self was in there.

The reason I love you and started loving you was your humor. That so attracted me to you. Because even when the hard times really started, we could still laugh at things.

I love that you are so beautiful.

I love watching you express your creativity down at the banquet hall and being in your element with all those parties you're throwing.

I love you for letting me make bad decisions at times and just rolling with it. And you know, you're just a safe place for me again. I hope I'm that for you.

You showed me that love was consistent, love was kind, and that love heals. I was expecting so many times for you to just walk away because I was trying to get away from myself. But you stayed. And you fought. And you saw something valuable in me that I didn't even believe. But you have made my life so rich. So rich.

I tell you all the time that without you, I'd be a hermit, just isolated somewhere. But you have made my life so interesting. You've made our life a roller coaster instead of a merry-go-round with highs and lows, ins and outs, and hairpin turns. But it's been so much fun. So much fun. I always tell you I can never divorce you because I would lose two-thirds of my memory if you weren't around to remind me of all the good stuff.

I am so grateful that you were willing to fight for us. That you were willing to love when I didn't even know what love was. I just didn't. I had some glimpses of it from Mama June and Bud, but I saw what love truly was looking through your eyes.

You're the reason that I find any happiness at all. And if I can make you happy at times, it makes me happy. I'm grateful that you chose me to spend your life with. I'm really grateful that you chose to believe I could grow up and become the kind of man you needed me to be.

For all these reasons and more, I do love you so. I really do.

—Russ

TO RUSS

I love you and I respect you because I watched you fight for me. It didn't always look like it a lot of times. But you did what it takes to earn back trust, and I respect that. There wasn't an easy way out of your addiction, and you did the hard work.

I love your heart. You have such an open welcoming heart.

You are the least judgmental person I've ever met. And you always ask the right question. When somebody's in front of us and they are behaving badly, I usually say, "What in the world is wrong with them?" But you ask the question, "I wonder what happened to them?" I love that you have taken what happened to you and are now able to extend that grace and compassion to other people. I really appreciate that about you.

I love that you went to all those parties that you didn't want to go to. I love that you never tried to change me. We used to joke about that you should have married a Pentecostal piano player. But I have never felt like you wanted me to be anybody other than me.

I love that you love our girls. You had no role model for what a healthy dad looks like. And somewhere, in the middle of the healing, you learned how to love those girls even more.

It's been a lot, hasn't it?

I'm so glad you're still here.

—Tori

BROKEN BEAUTIFULLY

Standing in the spotlight makes it hard to see the cracks
But even with my eyes closed, I can trace each line and track
Living in the shadows only widens all the gaps
But when I drag myself towards daylight,
I feel your hand upon my back,
I can't help but wonder as I struggle to my knees
How many more are out there
Broken beautifully like me?

Rain falls on the water, it doesn't leave a mark,
Pain pushes to the surface, it can scar the strongest heart,
Sometimes healing takes a different path
Than what you thought it'd be
God makes art from pieces that are broken beautifully

Sidestepping the bruised and battered edges of my soul
Tiptoeing through minefields, ever mindful of my role
Wondering why the accolades don't fill the gaping hole
If I can keep the giant sleeping, no one ever has to know.
I wasted so much precious time determined not to see
And now with eyes wide open
I'm broken beautifully, but free.

Jagged little fragments, mountains cleft in two
Our wreckage is his canvas, love and grace in every hue

(Lyrics by Tori Taff)

SPECIAL THANKS

Russ and Tori would like to thank Mark Smeby for his unparalleled writing skills, wide-open heart, and blessedly inappropriate humor. An intimidating process turned into an unexpectedly rich and enjoyable experience because of your generous collaboration. What a gift you are. To Rick Altizer and Kent Songer, who first believed this was a story worth telling. To Michael Wilson and Post Hill Press for making our most deeply held dream a reality. To our families for loving us, our friends for supporting us, the small army of skilled therapists for teaching us, and for recovery communities everywhere for giving hurting people a place to heal.

Mark Smeby would like to thank Russ and Tori for the incomparable joy this project has been, and for allowing me into their lives and showing me the power of love and grace, and the importance of getting professional help. I'll always remember hearing the vulnerability of the lyrics you two wrote, especially on the *Walls of Glass* record, and feeling way less abnormal than I was convinced I was. To Michael Wilson for this opportunity and your belief in me since

Maryland Farms days. To Anthony, Michael, and the awesome crew at Post Hill Press for the incredible work you do to make us all look better than we are. To Rick Altizer for the beautiful film you made and the incredible amount of help you gave me with this book. To my family for your beautiful, generous love that has made me who I am—I'm eternally grateful.